cruelty by nature

THE SCIENCE OF INTENTIONAL ABUSE

DR. PETER SALERNO

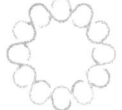

To my wife—who endured unimaginable cruelty in childhood, yet chose to live with dignity, compassion, and unwavering respect for all beings. You are living proof that those who suffer immeasurable harm need not perpetuate harm themselves. Your strength, integrity, and kindness inspire me every day.

contents

acknowledgments

I am deeply grateful to those who have supported and sustained me throughout the writing of this book. To my wife and family, whose love and encouragement have been my foundation. To my mentors and colleagues, who have guided and challenged me. To the trailblazers who are advancing a paradigm shift in how we understand and educate about intentional abuse. To the science-minded experts who value truth above ego and are unafraid to be proven wrong in the pursuit of knowledge. To the advocates who tirelessly seek justice for survivors. And above all, to the survivors themselves, who have entrusted me with their lived experiences and who have found strength and clarity in my work. This book is offered in gratitude to all of you.

about the author

Peter Salerno, PsyD, is a Doctor of Psychology, retired licensed psychotherapist and nationally recognized expert on personality disorders and pathological relationships. He has received specialized training in both trauma treatment and the assessment of personality disorders and has been trained in the administration and scoring of the Hare Psychopathy Checklist–Revised (PCL-R), the global standard for evaluating psychopathy in clinical and forensic settings. Dr. Salerno specializes in the psychological assessment of personality pathology and recovery from pathological relationship abuse. He is the author of "Traumatic Cognitive Dissonance" and "The Nature and Nurture of Narcissism" and is a featured expert in the Hulu series "Ted Bundy: Dialogue with the Devil." His work integrates cutting-edge research with practical, trauma-informed education for both survivors and clinicians.

Website: drpetersalerno.com
Instagram: @drpetersalerno
YouTube: @DrPeterSalerno

preface

FOR OVER A century, psychology has sought to explain cruelty through the lenses available to it — myth and moral metaphor, psychoanalytic narrative, adversity theory, sociological accounts, behaviorist models of learned aggression, and cognitive theories of distorted thinking and moral failure. These frameworks carried cultural resonance and gave language to suffering. They also softened judgment, promising that if we understood the pain behind abusive behavior, redemption was possible. But while these perspectives opened the door to empathy, they too often closed the door on truth. They minimized survivors' testimony, excused deliberate harm, and obscured the deeper roots of personality pathology.

The time has come for psychology to evolve. Advances in behavioral genetics and neuroscience have illuminated what earlier models overlooked: abuse functions as a deliberate strategy grounded in stable personality traits such as callousness, aggression, entitlement, and manipulation. These traits are not imagined, nor are they simply "learned"; they are measurable, heritable, and expressed through brain systems regulating empathy, aggression, and impulse control. To ignore these findings is to remain tethered to sentiment at the expense of science.

This book is written at a critical turning point—a moment when we must shift the zeitgeist of psychology. A new framework is needed, one that values the insights of past theorists yet refuses to stop where they left off. By grounding our understanding of abuse in the biological underpinnings of personality, we not only sharpen science but also honor survivors of intentional abuse and coercion. For too long, their accounts of deliberate cruelty were dismissed as exaggeration or misperception. The evidence now confirms what survivors have always known: abuse is intentional, instrumental, and patterned.

To confront this reality is not to abandon compassion. It is to restore moral clarity. When we see abuse as strategy rather than accident, we validate the lived experiences of those who endured it. When we integrate biology with psychology, we strengthen the field itself—bringing it into alignment with the broader sciences of human behavior. And when we hold abusers accountable, we move society toward justice rather than rationalization.

This is the task before us: to expand psychology

beyond excuses and toward truth. If this work contributes to that shift—if it gives survivors recognition, clinicians a clearer framework, and society a firmer grasp of accountability—then it has done its part in shaping the next chapter of our understanding of human cruelty.

PART I

THE SCIENCE OF CRUELTY

nature's architecture:
The Genetic Foundations of Personality Pathology

The Long Shadow of Environmental Determinism

THE FIELD OF psychology has historically explained the behavior of abusers, manipulators, and controllers through a single enduring assumption: *hurt people hurt people*. The belief that abusive behavior is simply the byproduct of unresolved childhood wounds has become a cultural truism, echoed in therapy rooms, self-help books, and social media posts alike. In this telling, the abuser is not so much malevolent as misguided—a "wounded child" trapped in an adult body, repeating cycles of pain they once endured.

This view is appealing for several reasons. It offers a clear villain—neglect, trauma, bad parenting—and a sympathetic explanation for destructive behavior. It allows us to imagine that if only the right wound could be healed, the abusive individual could become *whole* again. Most of all, it reassures us that such darkness is not innate to the human condition—that it is imposed from without, not woven from within. By attributing abusive behavior to damage rather than disposition, society can preserve the comforting belief that cruelty has an external origin.

Yet science tells a far more complicated story. Over the past few decades, advances in behavioral genetics, neuroscience, neurobiology, and evolutionary psychology have revealed that personality traits—including those underlying severe personality pathology—are *highly innate* and *biologically based*, rather than primarily shaped by environmental influences. Research with twins and adoptees demonstrates that traits such as aggression, manipulativeness, grandiosity, callousness, impulsivity, exploitation, and lack of empathy appear early in development, mature naturally across the lifespan, and are driven more by genetic differences than by environmental responses. These traits *do not* require trauma to appear; rather, they reflect biological differences in temperament, brain circuitry, and genetic architecture. Unlike the common but misleading metaphor that genes "load the gun" and environment "pulls the trigger," research shows that DNA is continuously active in shaping personality regardless of whether trauma is present.

This is not to say that environment is completely irrelevant. Trauma can and does exacerbate vulnerabilities, and supportive environments may in some cases buffer them. But the evidence is clear: *trauma is neither necessary nor sufficient to cause a personality disorder.* Many survivors of profound abuse emerge with no personality pathology, while others possess disordered traits despite stable, loving upbringings. Genes and environment are constantly interacting, but the old deterministic view—that trauma alone "creates" abusers—does not hold up under scrutiny.

This reframing has enormous implications for how we understand pathological abusive behavior. If we continue to explain abuse solely as the product of "woundedness," we risk minimizing the intentionality behind manipulation, coercion, and control. We overlook the evidence that many individuals choose strategies of exploitation, deceit, and domination because these strategies serve them. The genetic and neurobiological roots of personality do not excuse these behaviors—but they help explain why such patterns are resistant to change, why they are not simply "misunderstandings," and why so many victims walk away from abusive relationships feeling that the cruelty was deliberate.

In this book, I argue for a new paradigm. Abusers are not broken children crying out for love; they are adults who employ tactics of control and manipulation rooted in enduring personality structures. Understanding this requires us to move beyond comforting myths and confront a darker truth: some individuals are wired toward exploitation, and their abuse cannot be explained away as the accidental consequence of suffering. Only by integrating genetics, neurobiology, and environmental influences into a comprehensive model can we understand pathological abuse for what it truly is—a pattern of behavior grounded in both nature and nurture, yet enacted with intent.

Behavioral Genetics

Behavioral genetics has fundamentally reshaped our understanding of personality, offering an empirically grounded counterweight to the environmental determinism of the twentieth century. Twin and adoption studies reveal that heritability estimates for personality traits range from 40% to 60%, indicating that much of the variability in traits such as manipulativeness, aggression, grandiosity, deceitfulness, and emotional reactivity can be traced to genetics rather than environment. Even when identical twins are raised apart, the inherent traits they share through genetic similarity predict strikingly parallel behavioral patterns, emotional temperaments, and interpersonal dynamics.

When these methods are applied to a particular group of disorders known as the Cluster B personality disorders, the findings are even more striking. In psychiatric classification, Cluster B refers to a family of disorders—narcissistic, borderline, antisocial, and histrionic—that share traits of emotional volatility, manipulation, and interpersonal exploitation. These are the disorders most closely associated with deliberate forms of cruelty explored throughout this book, manifesting primarily through attempts to control, manipulate, or emotionally dominate others.

Heritability estimates for these disorders routinely exceed 60%, with some studies placing narcissistic personality disorder as high as 79%, borderline personality disorder at 69%, and antisocial personality disorder also near 69%. Histrionic personality disorder demonstrates substantial heritability as well—approximately 67% in twin samples—underscoring how deeply entrenched these temperamental predispositions can be.

Equally significant are the findings that *shared family environment* contributes little to the development of severe personality pathology. Identical twins reared apart often display more similarity than fraternal twins reared together. Adoption studies mirror these results: children tend to resemble their biological parents in personality more closely than their adoptive ones. The implication is profound—"the home alone" cannot account for the emergence of enduring maladaptive traits. Instead, heritable dispositions and *nonshared environments*—those idiosyncratic experiences shaped by a child's unique biology, perceptions, and interactions—dominate the picture.

At the molecular level, genome-wide association studies (GWAS) provide converging evidence for the genetic basis of personality pathology. Large-scale meta-analyses of traits linked to Cluster B pathology—such as antagonism, disinhibition, and negative affectivity—have identified thousands of single nucleotide polymorphisms

(SNPs), each exerting a small but additive influence. Recent GWAS indicate that polygenic risk scores for negative affectivity and emotional dysregulation predict borderline personality features, while scores related to externalizing behaviors—traits involving impulsivity and disinhibition—show associations across antisocial, narcissistic, and borderline spectra. Together, these findings confirm that personality disorders are not random accidents of upbringing but complex polygenic architectures unfolding through lifelong interactions with environment and temperament.

Neurobiology

Neurobiology has further clarified the biological mechanisms underlying personality. The brain, far from being a blank slate molded by parental behavior, exhibits consistent structural and functional differences in individuals with severe personality pathology. Circuits governing empathy, impulse control, and emotional regulation are especially implicated. Dysfunctions in pathways connecting the prefrontal cortex, amygdala, and anterior cingulate cortex disrupt regulation of affect and inhibition, while alterations in the insula compromise empathy and interoceptive awareness.

These neural findings are mirrored by abnormalities in neurotransmitter and hormonal systems. Dysregulation of serotonin and dopamine contributes to sensation-seeking and impulsivity; imbalances in norepinephrine heighten emotional volatility; and disturbances in oxytocin and cortisol signaling interfere with bonding, stress adaptation, and threat sensitivity. Such biological variations cannot be meaningfully reduced to "learned behavior." Instead, they represent enduring differences in neural architecture and neurochemical tone that predispose certain individuals toward specific emotional and interpersonal patterns.

Collectively, behavioral genetics and neurobiology converge on the same conclusion: severe personality pathology reflects *intrinsic differences* in brain organization and function, not simply the psychological scars of early experience.

Trauma Without Determinism

None of this negates the profound impact of trauma. Adverse experiences—abuse, neglect, and deprivation—can intensify existing vulnerabilities, alter developmental trajectories, and compound emotional risk. Yet trauma is neither necessary nor sufficient to produce a personality disorder. Research demonstrates that many children exposed to severe abuse develop no enduring pathology. Among siblings raised in the same environment, one may develop a personality disorder while another does not. Conversely, disordered traits often appear in individuals with no notable trauma history.

This asymmetry reflects the principle of gene–environment interaction: genetic propensities influence how we perceive and respond to life events. Some individuals are biologically sensitive to environmental adversity, while others remain comparatively unaffected or resilient. Trauma can serve as a catalyst in genetically susceptible individuals, but it does not explain the phenomenon of personality disorder in its entirety. The presence of trauma in a person's past does not automatically transform cruelty into a symptom; it may simply provide context for how an already vulnerable temperament expressed itself over time.

Consider two siblings raised by the same abusive parent. One may develop narcissistic traits—entitlement, lack of empathy, and manipulation—while the other becomes conscientious, compassionate, and protective of others. The difference lies not merely in parental treatment but in temperament. Each child's genetic constitution interacts uniquely with the same environment, eliciting different parental responses and shaping distinct internal narratives. Nonshared environmental factors—those experiences unique to each child—account for far more variance in outcome than shared ones. This underscores a critical reality: parenting, though influential, is not powerful enough to dictate destiny.

Patterns Too Consistent to Ignore

Across cultures, socioeconomic classes, and generations, certain behavioral patterns emerge with striking consistency. The same repertoire of manipulation, dominance, and emotional exploitation manifests in individuals who have never met, shared an upbringing, or lived in comparable environments. This cross-cultural uniformity undermines the notion that cruelty is learned exclusively through adversity. Instead, it suggests a stable and biologically influenced architecture of personality—one that, under certain configurations, predisposes to cruelty.

When these recurrent patterns are viewed through the lens of behavioral genetics, their consistency makes sense. If traits like impulsivity, callousness, and emotional instability are heritable, it follows that similar constellations of behavior would appear repeatedly, regardless of environment. Such repetition is not coincidence—it arises from the genetic architecture underlying personality.

Abuse as Strategy, Not Symptom

Understanding the genetic and neurobiological underpinnings of personality has profound implications for how we interpret abusive behavior. It reframes abuse as a product of enduring traits rather than as the residue of past pain, explaining why many abusers remain unrepentant or indifferent to the harm they cause. Their behavior reflects stable dispositions rather than temporary maladaptive defenses. This recognition cautions against trauma-only models that risk excusing deliberate cruelty as the unintended consequence of suffering.

When viewed through this lens, manipulation,

exploitation, and control are not random acts of emotional chaos but intentional strategies. Reality distortion, domination, and emotional degradation serve instrumental aims: to gain power, reassurance, or control. These patterns persist not because they are unconscious, but because they are effective—and neurologically rewarding.

This understanding challenges the popular belief that all cruelty is a symptom of pain—that only the wounded harm others, and that they only do so because they have been harmed. While all humans are capable of acting from pain, individuals with entrenched Cluster B traits operate from a more complex calculus. Their aggression and exploitation are not necessarily reactions to distress but reflections of personality systems optimized for dominance, self-enhancement, and personal advantage. Such behaviors resist change not because insight is impossible, but because they are woven into the fabric of temperament and reinforced by experience.

Recognizing abuse as strategy rather than symptom clarifies both prevention and recovery. It protects victims from misattributing malice to misunderstanding and reorients therapeutic expectations toward realism rather than reform. Compassion remains essential, but it must coexist with discernment; empathy without boundaries invites re-victimization. Seeing abuse clearly means acknowledging that cruelty is not a defense mechanism to excuse but a choice to condemn.

A Roadmap for What Follows

This book expands upon three interrelated themes introduced here.

First, *the science of personality*—its genetic and neurobiological foundations—demonstrates the limits of environmental determinism and the need to recognize the enduring biological architecture of temperament. Second, *the myth of trauma as destiny* is dismantled through empirical evidence showing that trauma neither guarantees pathology nor explains cruelty. And third, *the intentionality of abuse* is explored in depth: manipulation and control are deliberate strategies rooted in enduring personality structures, not accidents of suffering.

Together, these themes form the foundation for a clearer, empirically grounded understanding of human cruelty—one that honors complexity without excusing harm, and that replaces comforting myths with the clarity of science.

two
the spectrum of the dramatic and the dangerous
The Evolution of Cluster B
Personality Disorders

WHEN MENTAL HEALTH professionals first began
cataloging personality patterns in the twentieth century,
they hoped to create a universal map of human behavior
—one that could distinguish eccentricity from pathology
and passion from peril. The *Diagnostic and Statistical
Manual of Mental Disorders*—the DSM—became that
map. By 1980, its third edition introduced a new organizational system: personality disorders arranged into three
clusters. Cluster A contained the odd or eccentric;
Cluster C described the anxious and fearful. Cluster B,
however, captured the volatile, the grandiose, the manipulative, and the emotionally combustible.

This cluster—comprising narcissistic, borderline,
histrionic, and antisocial personalities—was united by a
kind of dramatic intensity. These individuals could
inspire fascination or fear, but always evoked strong reaction. Their behavior was not merely erratic; it was strate-

gic. Cluster B traits involved not only emotion without restraint, but emotion deployed as a weapon. The cruelty that emerged from this cluster was often deliberate, rooted not in confusion but in intention—the capacity to recognize what hurts and to use that knowledge.

From Sin to Science

Long before the DSM codified these conditions, philosophers and early physicians observed people who seemed sane in reason yet deranged in morality. In 1801, Philippe Pinel wrote of patients suffering from "mania without delirium"—individuals who could think clearly while committing acts of shocking callousness. James Cowles Prichard followed with the term *moral insanity*, describing those whose intellect remained intact but whose conscience seemed absent. Their cruelty was cold, measured, and purposeful. It was not madness but a moral deformity—what today we might call psychopathy.

In the twentieth century, psychoanalysis attempted to humanize this darkness. Freud's theories placed destructive impulses within a broader struggle between instinct and conscience. Otto Kernberg later described narcissistic and borderline personalities as trapped in primitive emotional worlds, where love and hate could not coexist. Heinz Kohut framed narcissism as a wound—a desperate compensation for developmental injury. These accounts softened our view of cruelty by recasting it as pain turned outward. But in doing so, psychology often lost sight of

something crucial: not all cruelty is a cry for help. Sometimes, it is a calculated method of control.

The DSM Era: Naming the Dangerous

By the 1980s, psychiatry sought to replace metaphor with
measurement. The DSM-III's categorical system trans-
formed personality pathology into a checklist of observable criteria. Traits like deceitfulness, grandiosity,
impulsivity, and lack of empathy became codified as
features. Clinicians finally had a diagnostic vocabulary for
the charming con artist, the volatile lover, the theatric
attention-seeker, and the entitled deceiver. Yet the clinical
language also sanitized the subject matter. Euphemisms
stood in for cruelty and indifference to suffering.

What appeared as diagnostic neutrality masked a
deeper truth. Many individuals fitting these descriptions
understood exactly what they were doing. Their harm
was not the product of confusion but of precision. They
could anticipate emotional responses, read vulnerability,
and manipulate outcomes to serve personal advantage.
The DSM described such patterns as "impairments in
empathy" and "interpersonal dysfunction," but in the
lived experience of victims, the distinction between
symptom and sadism blurred. Cruelty, in this sense, was
not an accident of temperament—it was a chosen
instrument.

When Cruelty Becomes Strategy

For decades, psychology clung to the narrative that abusers are simply damaged people reenacting their own pain. The idea that "hurt people hurt people" became a cultural reflex. Yet empirical research has since complicated this moral comfort. Studies on Cluster B personalities reveal that many possess normal—or even heightened—cognitive empathy. They can read others with remarkable accuracy. What is impaired is affective empathy: the emotional resonance that gives meaning to another's suffering. This division allows for manipulation without remorse.

In these personalities, cruelty becomes a form of mastery—employed to establish dominance, punish perceived slights, or sustain self-importance. The behavior may appear impulsive from the outside, but its timing often reveals calculation. Affection becomes ammunition; attachment invites discard. These are not random reactions but patterned performances—scripts designed to maintain control through alternating reward and punishment.

Traits, Not Types

As the field evolved, the idea of personality disorders as fixed categories began to fracture. Clinicians noticed that individuals rarely fit neatly into one box. A narcissistic patient might also show borderline volatility; an antisocial one might display histrionic flair for dramatization. In response, researchers shifted toward a dimensional view of personality, emphasizing traits rather than labels.

The DSM's later editions introduced the concept of maladaptive trait domains such as Antagonism, Disinhibition, Negative Affectivity, and Detachment. The World Health Organization's *ICD-11* also added a dimensional, severity-based model for personality disorders. Within this dimensional framework, cruelty is understood as a product of high antagonism—traits that include deceit, arrogance, and callousness—combined with low conscientiousness and emotional regulation.

These dimensional models reveal that the architecture of cruelty is not mysterious. It arises from recognizable combinations of temperament: dominance without empathy, exploitation without restraint, and entitlement without self-reflection. These traits exist in the normal population, but when amplified by problematic biological underpinnings, they consolidate into enduring strategies of cruelty.

The Shift to Science

Modern research supports this view with evidence from genetics and neuroscience. Twin studies show that traits associated with Cluster B disorders are moderately to highly heritable. Brain imaging reveals diminished activity in areas responsible for empathy and moral reasoning, alongside heightened activation in reward circuits tied to aggression and dominance. These findings suggest that certain individuals are biologically predisposed toward emotional coldness or impulsive control, though predisposition does not equal destiny.

Behavioral genetics reframes the question of intent. If temperament shapes perception and impulse, then cruelty may emerge not from ignorance but from a skewed calculus—an inherited bias toward self-interest. In these individuals, power feels better than intimacy, and control feels better than connection.

Evolution's Reluctant Legacy

Evolutionary psychology extends this view beyond pathology into the origins of human nature. The same traits that destroy trust in modern society—manipulation, deception, dominance—once conferred survival advantages. In small ancestral groups, cunning could secure food, status, or mates. Those who could read and exploit others sometimes thrived more readily than those who cooperated. Nature, indifferent to morality, preserved both strategies: empathy and exploitation.

Cruelty, then, may represent an evolutionary surplus —a trait that once offered advantage but now undermines social cohesion. It persists because it works in the short term, even as it corrodes the long term. Cluster B disorders reveal what happens when social intelligence operates without empathy—when the capacity to understand others is used to exploit rather than connect.

The Theatre of Intent

Across all frameworks—categorical, dimensional, biological, or evolutionary—the defining feature of Cluster B pathology is the conscious manipulation of others. These individuals do not merely react to emotion; they direct it. The narcissistic personality wounds to assert superiority. The antisocial personality deceives to dominate. The borderline personality lashes out not blindly, but often with acute awareness of where the blow will land hardest. The histrionic personality performs emotion to maintain attention, shaping others' responses with practiced skill.

Each knows what they are doing at some level. They can see you clearly enough to wound you precisely. It is this intentional quality—this choreography of harm—that separates ordinary dysfunction from the pathology of predation.

Culture as Amplifier

Modern culture amplifies these traits on a mass scale. Social media rewards exhibitionism; business celebrates ruthlessness; politics prizes dominance over dialogue. The line between pathology and success blurs when charisma and manipulation become indistinguishable from leadership. The narcissistic pursuit of admiration and the antisocial pursuit of advantage now operate under the guise of ambition. What should be pathologized, society increasingly normalizes.

This cultural mirror matters, because it reveals how environmental conditions can amplify innate traits. Just as empathy thrives in cooperative systems, cruelty flourishes in competitive ones. The same traits that destroy relationships can be rewarded in economies built on self-promotion and control. Cluster B personalities do not simply defy culture—they reflect its values in their most extreme form.

Why Intent Matters

Understanding the role of intention reshapes how we think about abuse. When harm is deliberate—when the abuser knows the effect of their actions and continues—it cannot be excused as mere dysfunction or illness. The cruelty of Cluster B personalities lies in that awareness. They injure not from confusion but from design.

This recognition restores moral clarity to psychological discourse. To understand does not mean to excuse. Science can explain how cruelty forms without diluting its meaning. It allows understanding of the origins of these traits while holding individuals accountable for their choices.

three
circuits of cruelty
The Neurobiology of Cluster B Personality Disorders

CLUSTER B PERSONALITY disorders are defined by patterns of dominance, manipulation, and emotional volatility that consistently unfold in social settings. These are not random lapses of judgment or sudden explosions of passion; they are predictable behaviors arising from measurable differences in brain structure, chemistry, and regulation.

Where Chapter Two examined the historical and dimensional framework of these disorders, this chapter moves beneath the surface—to the circuitry and chemistry that make them possible. Understanding intentional cruelty requires tracing how the brain's architecture encodes patterns of empathy, dominance, and reward.

Circuits of Cluster B Pathology

Each Cluster B disorder reflects a distinctive neural signature, revealing how emotional regulation and moral awareness diverge from the norm.

In Narcissistic Personality Disorder (NPD), the dysfunction resides in circuits governing self-focus and empathy. Studies reveal reduced gray matter in the anterior insula, anterior cingulate cortex (ACC), and dorsolateral and medial prefrontal cortex (PFC)—regions crucial for integrating self-referential thought with emotional attunement. Disrupted white-matter connectivity across fronto-thalamic and long association tracts further impairs self-regulation, correlating directly with pathological narcissism severity. Functionally, reduced activation in the right anterior insula during empathy tasks suggests a selective disengagement from others' emotions. The result is not emotional blindness, but emotional detachment—a mind capable of understanding others but unwilling to integrate their experience. This circuitry underlies the hallmark features of narcissistic cruelty: calculated manipulation, shallow empathy, and self-referential dominance.

In psychopathy, the amygdala—crucial for fear learning and moral evaluation—shows reduced volume and reactivity. The uncinate fasciculus, the white-matter tract connecting the amygdala to the ventromedial prefrontal cortex (vmPFC), is weakened, diminishing the brain's capacity to link threat cues with moral inhibition. The result is an emotional disconnection from consequences. Neuroimaging reveals paralimbic dysfunction and hypoactivation of moral-inhibition circuits during empathy or punishment tasks. These deficits manifest behaviorally as fearlessness, instrumental aggression, and emotional coldness—the ingredients of cruelty devoid of conscience.

Borderline Personality Disorder (BPD) offers a contrasting picture. Rather than emotional detachment, BPD is marked by emotional overactivation. Neuroimaging studies reveal smaller amygdala and hippocampal volumes, findings consistent with heightened stress reactivity and unstable mood regulation. White-matter disruptions between limbic and prefrontal regions weaken top-down control. Functionally, the amygdala is hyperreactive to *perceived* social threat and rejection cues, triggering intense fear of abandonment and erratic attempts to prevent it. The resulting emotional storms are not simply mood swings— they are neurobiologically driven responses to perceived relational danger. Where psychopathy suppresses empathy, borderline pathology amplifies threat and demand. Both distort connection, but from opposite directions.

The Chemistry That Biases Behavior

Neural circuits provide the structure of personality; neurotransmitters and hormones provide the propulsion.

Together, they tilt the brains of Cluster B personalities toward dominance and volatility.

Serotonin functions as a behavioral brake, dampening impulsivity and aggression. Low serotonergic tone —found consistently in antisocial and borderline pathology—removes that restraint, allowing violent or erratic impulses to break through.

Dopamine, conversely, drives reward, novelty-seeking, and dominance. Elevated or dysregulated dopamine signaling promotes entitlement, thrill-seeking, and exploitation—patterns common in narcissistic and psychopathic personalities.

Other neurochemicals, including noradrenaline, GABA, and glutamate, further modulate vigilance and inhibition. When these systems misfire, emotional regulation becomes precarious and arousal levels unpredictable, setting the stage for volatility and aggression.

Hormonal systems layer yet another dimension onto this biology. Cortisol, regulated by the hypothalamic–pituitary–adrenal (HPA) axis, reflects how individuals respond to stress. In BPD, exaggerated cortisol reactivity corresponds with emotional storms and difficulty returning to baseline. In psychopathy, the opposite occurs —chronically blunted cortisol activity corresponds with fearlessness and punishment insensitivity.

Oxytocin, often celebrated as the "bonding hormone," behaves paradoxically in these disorders. In BPD, oxytocin release heightens mistrust and emotional volatility, amplifying sensitivity to perceived rejection. In exploitative personalities, oxytocin signaling may serve strategic ends—facilitating charm and superficial bonding without genuine emotional reciprocity. These patterns reinforce the relational paradox of Cluster B pathology: relationships that imitate attachment but are manipulative, volatile, and instrumental rather than empathic.

Prenatal Programming vs. Heritable Biology

Some critics argue that these neurobiological patterns can be explained by prenatal stress. Elevated maternal cortisol, for instance, may influence fetal development through the placenta. But while prenatal environments *affect* sensitivity, they do not create enduring patterns of personality pathology.

First, genetic variation in neurotransmitter and receptor systems—such as polymorphisms in the serotonin transporter (5-HTTLPR) and dopamine receptor (DRD4, DRD2) genes—exists prior to any environmental input. Second, the same prenatal conditions often yield different outcomes among siblings, reflecting genetic variation more than environmental influence. Third, gene–environment interactions—demonstrated in classic behavioral-genetic studies—show that environmental stressors amplify vulnerability only in those who are genetically predisposed.Finally, the stability of personality traits across decades and contexts points to a genetic–neurobiological architecture, not a transient prenatal effect.

Prenatal stress may modulate, to some degree, the expression of these predispositions but cannot account for the enduring predictability of cruelty, deceit, and dominance. Biology provides the blueprint; the environment—womb included—merely colors some of its expression.

Enduring Systems, Intentional Strategies

The convergence of brain imaging, neurotransmitter studies, and hormonal research leads to a clear conclusion: the machinery of cruelty is stable. Reduced serotonergic restraint, elevated dopaminergic drive, and blunted cortisol responses reinforce behaviors of dominance and reward-seeking. Hyperreactive limbic circuits amplify volatility, while weak prefrontal governance fails to moderate it. These systems generate consistent behavioral patterns—exploitation, manipulation, and control—that repeat despite insight or intervention.

Cruelty, in this light, is not a symptom of chaos but an organized system of strategies. It arises from neural and chemical configurations that bias the brain toward exploitation, not empathy; toward control, not connection.

The stability of these patterns explains why abusers

repeat familiar tactics and why remorse so often serves as a means of persuasion rather than a sign of change. These findings do not strip responsibility from the individual— they define it. Intentionality in cruelty reflects the conscious use of evolved capacities for harm—the ability to recognize suffering and inflict it deliberately.

four
the seduction of a tragic story
Why Environments Do Not Design Abusers

THE IDEA THAT trauma or environmental adversity is the root of all personality pathology is now woven into both clinical language and popular culture. Therapists often frame personality disorders as maladaptive responses to early abuse or neglect; self-help literature echoes the belief that those who suffer simply pass their suffering on. The story is compelling because it offers a single cause, an object of sympathy, and a path to redemption through healing. It grants us the relief of a moral shortcut: if cruelty is a scar, then compassion alone should cure it.

But the science tells a harder, more interesting story. Not all abused children develop personality pathology, and not all people with severe pathology experience abuse. Trauma is influential, but it is not destiny. The clinical implication is sobering: cruelty frequently emerges not from a wound that needs soothing, but from a temperament that weaponizes social knowledge.

Risk Factors Are Not Causes

Adverse childhood experiences (ACEs) increase the *likelihood* of later emotional or behavioral problems, but they do not *cause* a specific personality disorder in any direct or linear way. Longitudinal and twin studies consistently show that early adversity predicts later difficulties primarily in those already temperamentally susceptible— high in negative affectivity, low in agreeableness, volatile under stress.

Interventions that buffer adversity often improve functioning but do not eliminate entrenched traits— particularly when those traits are strongly heritable. In borderline personality disorder, for instance, the popular belief that severe trauma is universal does not hold. Research shows that only about one-third of individuals with BPD report early trauma, a meaningful minority of cases. Many others describe chronic feelings of invalidation, rejection, or neglect—experiences interpreted through a biologically influenced temperament *biased* toward sensitivity, negativity, and perceived injury.

At the opposite end of the spectrum, many individuals high in narcissistic or psychopathic features describe stable, loving upbringings. Their lifelong fantasies of dominance, exploitation, or sadism require no narrative of pain to explain them; they reflect a design tilted toward power and away from empathy.

These observations do not minimize suffering. They refine the causal map. Adversity can accelerate or sharpen maladaptive trajectories, but without an underlying predisposition, it does not reliably produce Cluster B pathology.

Why Trauma-Only Models Persist

If trauma-only explanations are empirically weak, why do they remain dominant in clinical training and public discourse? One reason is that they are emotionally satisfying: they translate cruelty into pain—and pain into a plan for healing. They are also easier to discuss in therapy than biology. Temperament can feel immovable; trauma feels fixable. Another reason lies in the limits of clinical education. Many practitioners receive minimal exposure to behavioral genetics, neuroscience, or advanced training in personality disorders. A single survey course in abnormal psychology often leaves graduates fluent in psychodynamic or attachment narratives but largely unfamiliar with heritability and neural circuitry. Finally, trauma-centered models are appealing because they relocate responsibility—away from the abuser's choices and onto parents, culture, or society.

The cost of this displacement is profound: it obscures intentionality. It risks recasting manipulation, coercion, and deception not as deliberate strategies, but as reflexes.

When Trauma Meets Biology

A more accurate frame is interaction, not replacement.
Trauma matters *through* biology. Genetic propensities
determine how strongly environmental signals are regis-
tered and internalized. Two siblings may endure the same
hardships yet diverge sharply because their genotypes—
and thus their stress systems and temperaments—differ.

This interaction model preserves compassion while
restoring moral clarity. It explains why some trauma
survivors remain hypervigilant yet kind, while others
become exploitative and cruel. It also clarifies treatment
expectations: a person may process their trauma successfully yet still require lifelong structure to manage a
temperament predisposed toward dominance or
volatility.

The Epigenetics Debate

Epigenetics is often invoked to rescue environmental
determinism—experience "switches on" bad genes or
silences good ones, engraving trauma into biology. The
truth is more constrained. Epigenetic modifications are
real and measurable, but typically small, variable, and
reversible. They operate *within* genetic boundaries; they
do not override them.

In human studies, early stress can influence hormonal
regulation and immune tone, but these effects generally
attenuate over time and have not been shown to create

fixed patterns of personality pathology. In short, epigenetics adjusts the volume of a melody largely composed by heredity—it does not write new music. Recognizing these limits punctures the myth without denying anyone's pain. Trauma is not irrelevant to personality; it is simply insufficient to produce a personality disorder.

Resilience, Vulnerability, and Callous– Unemotional Pathways

In nearly every family touched by trauma, one haunting question emerges: why do some children bear deep psychological scars while others emerge relatively unscathed? The contrast reveals the importance of temperament and gene–environment interplay. Three developmental pathways illustrate this divergence.

Resilience: Born to Withstand Adversity

Resilience is often portrayed as grit or strong social support, but research shows it is substantially innate. Some children possess nervous systems less reactive to stress; they recover faster and regulate emotion more effectively. Executive functioning and adaptive regulation —capacities with clear heritable underpinnings—help these individuals maintain stability even in harsh environments. Resilience, then, is both taught and inherited: an inborn buffer that shapes how experience is processed and damage deflected.

Vulnerability: Sensitivity to Environment

At the other extreme are children biologically predisposed to intense emotionality. They respond to stress with heightened arousal—rapid hormonal activation, elevated heart rate, and slow recovery. In these individuals, adversity amplifies risk; instability interacts with innate sensitivity. In supportive environments, this same sensitivity may foster empathy or creativity—but the vulnerability remains. The *differential susceptibility* model explains this dual potential: the same genes that confer risk under stress can enhance adaptation in safety.

Importantly, high sensitivity is not synonymous with pathology. Empathic and creative individuals may feel deeply yet remain compassionate and stable, whereas borderline pathology often includes hostility, perceptual distortion, vengefulness, and chronic distrust—traits absent in the sensitive but healthy person.

Callous–Unemotional Traits: Stress Immunity and Indifference

A third pathway reflects the opposite pattern—low reactivity. Children high in callous–unemotional traits display shallow affect, low empathy, and indifference to distress. They appear unshakable because threat cues barely register. Research shows these traits are strongly heritable and observable early, often before significant trauma could have occurred. These are not wounded empaths turned cold; they are constitutionally indifferent. Their biology makes caring itself alien, and relationships become instruments of control rather than connection.

The Gene–Environment Equation

Resilience, vulnerability, and callousness reveal the same principle: genes and environment intertwine. Some children are like dandelions—adaptable across conditions. Others are like orchids—sensitive yet capable of remarkable growth under ideal care. Still others are like cacti—self-contained, needing little, giving little. The metaphor captures reality: outcomes are not dictated by adversity alone but filtered through temperament and biology.

Understanding these developmental pathways clarifies why abusive behavior is so consistent. Predispositions are not sentences, but they are constraints. The task of treatment—and of culture—is to design systems that make prosocial choice more rewarding than predation. Retiring the myth of the environment-made abuser allows accountability without injustice—and compassion without illusion.

PART II

RELATIONAL CRUELTY

five
entitled to cruelty
Narcissistic Personalities

The Mirage of Narcissism in Popular Culture

FEW PSYCHOLOGICAL TERMS have traveled as far—or been misunderstood as profoundly—as *narcissism.* Popular media frames it as vanity, arrogance, or insecurity wrapped in charm. Self-help culture warns of "low self-esteem beneath the grandiosity," suggesting that the narcissist's cruelty masks secret shame. But clinical literature tells a different story.

There is no *hidden reservoir* of low self-esteem inside the narcissist. Research confirms that what the DSM describes as "fragile self-esteem" does not mean the narcissist suffers from low self-worth. Rather, it refers to the *thinness* of their self-structure—the reliance on image instead of substance. Their sense of identity depends entirely on external reflection, like Narcissus gazing at his own image on the surface of the pond. The reflection is fragile not because it hides depth, but because it has none.

This distinction matters. Fragile self-esteem is the *result* of an incomplete self, not the cause of it. As many experts have emphasized, narcissistic pathology represents a failure of internal cohesion, not wounded self-confidence. While myths of hidden insecurity persist, the empirical evidence is consistent: narcissism is a disorder of *entitlement and exploitation,* not of inferiority. It is therefore a disorder of cruelty, strategy, and control.

This book cannot hope to extinguish every misconception about narcissism, but it can reveal what the science has long clarified—narcissistic cruelty is not reactive pain; it is deliberate domination.

Beyond Vanity

Narcissistic Personality Disorder (NPD) is not simply a matter of arrogance or self-importance. At its core lies a personality architecture built around entitlement, image maintenance, and interpersonal control. The narcissistic individual does not merely crave admiration; admiration is experienced as a *psychological necessity*—a steady infusion of exaltation that sustains their self-structure.

When admiration is abundant, the narcissist can appear magnetic, persuasive, even benevolent. But benevolence is conditional. It dissolves the moment superiority is threatened. What follows is a predictable pattern of cruelty, belittlement, and calculated exploitation that reveals the disorder's darker design.

Narcissistic cruelty is not impulsive chaos but *intentional strategy.* Over years, the narcissist refines methods of manipulation and coercion that destabilize those closest to them. Understanding these patterns requires examining the triad that defines the disorder: entitlement, image maintenance, and exploitative control.

Entitlement

Entitlement in NPD is not a passing belief that one "deserves more." It is a structural conviction that others exist to serve psychological and material needs. This orientation is visible early in development and cannot form without the genetic predispositions that incline a child toward dominance, arrogance, and low empathy.

By adulthood, entitlement manifests as a worldview in which relationships are hierarchical rather than reciprocal. Even mild opposition triggers disproportionate retaliation. Victims describe how refusals or boundaries provoke rage, devaluation, or contempt—punishments designed to restore dominance. The narcissist does not interpret "no" as a limit but as betrayal, an assault on the natural order. Cruelty functions as correction.

Image Maintenance

If entitlement governs expectations, image maintenance governs existence. The narcissistic self is a mask—an elaborate construction designed to sustain admiration and conceal emptiness. Feigned collaboration and superficial charm are tools of exploitation, not genuine connection.

Any threat to this image—criticism, exposure, loss of admiration—triggers aggressive countermeasures. Public humiliation, calculated withdrawal, or sudden devaluation of allies all serve one purpose: to preserve the idealized self. The mask must never slip, for beneath it lies not shame but void. The fragility of that void explains the ferocity of the reaction.

Manipulative Invalidation and Reality Distortion

Among the most psychologically corrosive tactics of narcissistic cruelty is manipulative invalidation, often described clinically as *reality distortion*. Narcissists do not simply disagree; they rewrite reality. Conversations are denied, facts inverted, perceptions ridiculed until the victim doubts their sanity.

This tactic fulfills several aims: it discredits the victim, reinforces the narcissist's role as the "arbiter of truth," and fosters dependence. Over time, victims lose confidence in their own perceptions and surrender to the narcissist's narrative. Such distortion is not confusion—it is precision. Each disavowal, each inversion of reality, serves domination.

Devaluation and Belittling

Devaluation is the signature act of narcissistic cruelty. It functions as a public performance of hierarchy and a private assertion of control. Subtle jabs, sarcasm, dismissive glances—these micro-acts accumulate until the victim's self-esteem erodes.

The cruelty lies in its persistence. One insult can wound; years of belittlement and devaluation can restructure identity. Victims describe feeling invisible, inadequate, or perpetually "not enough," even when objectively successful. Narcissistic cruelty is cumulative degradation—the slow rewriting of another's worth.

The Pursuit and Destruction of Intimacy

Research consistently shows that narcissists depend on attention yet recoil from genuine intimacy. Intimacy demands reciprocity, vulnerability, and equality—conditions incompatible with superiority.

Thus, narcissistic relationships oscillate between pursuit and sabotage. The partner is idealized, flooded with attention, and then gradually devalued once emotional closeness forms. Genuine intimacy threatens exposure of the narcissist's reliance on image, so they destroy what they cannot control. The result is a repetitive cycle of romantic captivation and emotional harm to the partner.

Cruelty as Strategy, Not Impulse

Unlike impulsive aggression in other disorders, narcissistic cruelty is deliberate and goal-oriented. It is refined through reinforcement: humiliation restores power, invalidation silences dissent, charm regains control.

A narcissistic executive may publicly undercut subordinates to reassert hierarchy; a romantic partner may withhold affection the moment autonomy emerges. These behaviors are not accidents but learned instruments—strategies rehearsed until they become instinctive.

Relational Aggression

Narcissists excel at covert relational aggression—indirect tactics that damage reputations, isolate targets, and maintain dominance within social hierarchies. Triangulation, gossip, and exclusion are standard tools. Romantic partners are manipulated through jealousy or emotional deprivation; colleagues through rivalry, sabotage, and deceit.

Once usefulness ends, individuals are often discarded with startling indifference. Victims often describe the "switch-flip" moment when affection vanishes and contempt takes its place. Relational aggression is not incidental to narcissism—it is its organizing strategy: a means of preserving control, asserting superiority, and managing the flow of admiration and submission within every relationship.

Cruelty Across Contexts

The pattern of domination transcends context. In families, narcissistic parents divide children into roles of "golden" and "scapegoat," enforcing lifelong imbalance. In workplaces, narcissistic leaders create toxic hierarchies built on fear and favoritism. Socially, they monopolize attention and devalue to elevate themselves.

Such consistency reveals structure, not circumstance. Narcissists are not situationally cruel—they are constitutionally cruel. Their need for control operates wherever hierarchy can be established.

The Victim's Experience

Survivors of pathological relationship abuse often describe an experience of cognitive and emotional disorientation. They feel magnetized and repelled simultaneously—drawn to charisma, trapped by contempt. Repeated cycles of idealization and rejection produce exhaustion, identity confusion, and trauma symptoms: hypervigilance, emotional numbing, mistrust, and loss of self-coherence.

These effects confirm that pathological relationship

abuse is not mere conflict; it is a sustained campaign of psychological coercion designed to break autonomy.

Why Cruelty Persists

Why does cruelty persist despite relational loss? Because it *works.* Each act of belittlement secures submission; each disavowal preserves power. In most environments—romantic, social, professional—narcissists face few consequences. Partners endure years before leaving; colleagues avoid confrontation; friends rationalize. Without accountability, cruelty becomes self-reinforcing.

Clinical and Cultural Implications

Clinically, understanding narcissistic cruelty as intentional rather than reactive is essential. Mental health professionals must resist framing narcissistic aggression as mere "acting out" or trauma repetition. Effective treatment requires confronting entitlement and enforcing accountability, not offering endless empathic validation.

Culturally, confronting narcissistic cruelty demands abandoning the comforting myth that abusers are simply wounded. Early adversity can influence development, but cruelty in narcissistic personality disorder reflects strategic dominance—not unconscious pain. Recognizing this reality protects victims, clarifies diagnosis, and dismantles narratives that excuse intentional harm.

Interpersonal cruelty in narcissism is not a glitch in

human nature—it is a blueprint for domination. Entitlement dictates expectation; image maintenance sustains illusion; exploitation secures control. To understand narcissism is to confront the chronicity of abuse itself. Recognition is the first step toward liberation; clarity, the first step toward accountability and justice.

six

cold, instrumental exploitation

Psychopathic and Antisocial
Personalities

PSYCHOPATHY HAS LONG captivated clinicians,
criminologists, and the general public—not only for its
association with violent crime, but for the chilling precision with which psychopaths exploit others. Unlike reactive forms of aggression, psychopathy is anticipatory. It
does not emerge in response to threat or conflict but
preempts it, manipulating circumstances to ensure dominance and control. Exploitation, in this sense, is not a
symptom but a strategy. The psychopath enacts cruelty as
a baseline mode of relating, approaching human interaction as a game of advantage. This distinction explains why
psychopathy occupies such a formidable place in the
study of personality pathology.

Weaponized Charm

Superficial charm remains among the most recognizable
hallmarks of psychopathy. Individuals high in psychopathic traits deploy charisma, wit, and apparent warmth
not as social skills, but as weapons. Their charm is instrumental—an entry point designed to disarm, seduce, and
secure access to others' trust. Victims frequently report
that their initial impressions were magnetic, even intoxicating. They recall being drawn to a sense of confidence
and ease that felt stabilizing. Only later do they discover
that the warmth was counterfeit, concealing indifference,
deception, or exploitation.

Deception is not incidental to psychopathy; it is
fundamental. Con artistry, fraud, and calculated deceit
represent not behavioral lapses but lifestyle strategies. In
these interactions, people are not partners or peers but
pawns—means to an end, used and discarded as conve-
nience dictates. What is most disturbing is not only the
manipulation, but the utter absence of guilt or remorse
that accompanies it. The psychopath's conscience is not
damaged—it is absent.

Callous–Unemotional Traits

At the psychological core of psychopathy are callous–
unemotional traits: the absence of guilt, empathy, or
remorse, and a willingness to inflict harm without hesita-

tion or regret. For most individuals, moral emotions such as shame, empathy, and guilt function as internal brakes against cruelty. The psychopath, by contrast, operates without these brakes. Their affective system is structurally indifferent to the suffering of others.

This emotional void explains their capacity for instrumental violence—harm committed not in the heat of anger but in the cool pursuit of gain. To external observers, such acts appear inhuman, as though the person were detached from basic moral awareness. Yet to the psychopath, cruelty is not emotionally charged; it is simply efficient. This difference—between moral horror and pragmatic action—defines the chilling essence of psychopathy.

Exploitation in Sexual and Romantic Life

Psychopathy often expresses itself in sexual and romantic domains through patterns of seduction, deceit, and betrayal. These individuals pursue short-term, exploitative relationships characterized by false intimacy and strategic manipulation. Romantic engagement is transactional—a stage for domination rather than connection.

Victims commonly describe a rapid sequence of idealization and betrayal. What begins as intoxicating attention soon reveals itself as hollow performance. Once trust is secured, empathy vanishes, replaced by cold indifference or deliberate cruelty. Psychopaths lack the neurological and emotional architecture required for genuine attachment. Their sexual lives reflect the same pattern found across all relationships: impersonal, controlling, and manipulative.

In some cases, this manipulation escalates into aggression or violence, especially when a partner resists control or exposes deceit. What emerges is not passion but predation—intimacy as a hunting ground.

Precision Over Passion

A defining feature distinguishing psychopathy from Antisocial Personality Disorder (ASPD) is composure. While antisocial individuals may erupt impulsively or act chaotically, the psychopath's cruelty is measured. Their emotional flatness serves as camouflage; they are not easily provoked, and when they display anger, it is often deliberate and rehearsed. Their aggression is not a loss of control but an assertion of it.

Robert Hare, whose pioneering work defined modern psychopathy, famously noted that psychopaths "know the words but not the music" of emotion. They can mimic empathy, simulate remorse, and recite the language of care, but these performances lack emotional resonance. The psychopath's understanding of emotion is cognitive, not affective; they study human feeling as a code to be exploited rather than an experience to be shared.

For victims, this detachment is particularly destabilizing. To be deceived by someone who appears empathic but is incapable of empathy fractures the foundations of trust. The trauma is not only interpersonal—it is existential, undermining belief in one's ability to perceive sincerity at all.

Strategic Exploitation

Psychopaths often demonstrate remarkable cognitive control when engaging in exploitation. Unlike impulsive offenders, they are capable of delaying gratification when patience enhances the payoff. This ability to suppress short-term impulses in pursuit of long-term manipulation underscores their strategic sophistication.

Victims frequently describe the chilling realization that they were *targeted*. Every confidence shared, every vulnerability revealed, becomes an asset in the psychopath's psychological ledger. The abuse of a psychopath is not chaotic; it is choreographed. Their cruelty operates with forethought, calibrated for maximum efficiency and minimum exposure. This calculated precision explains why many psychopaths function successfully in non-criminal contexts—corporate, political, or social—where charm and manipulation yield tangible rewards.

Psychopathy and Antisocial Personality Disorder

Although psychopathy and Antisocial Personality Disorder share features, they are not synonymous. The DSM-5-TR defines psychopathy as a specifier within ASPD, acknowledging that not all antisocial individuals are psychopathic.

ASPD emphasizes overt behavioral patterns—criminality, aggression, deceit, and irresponsibility—often driven by impulsivity. Psychopathy, by contrast, centers on enduring traits: callousness, superficial charm, and emotional detachment. Antisocial individuals may burn bridges in their chaos, but psychopaths cross them elegantly and on schedule. They do not merely break rules; they rewrite them in their favor.

This distinction has profound implications for understanding cruelty. While antisocial personalities are reckless, psychopaths are controlled. Their violence is colder, their manipulation more surgical, their exploitation more sustained. The absence of emotional reactivity is not weakness—it is weaponization of calm.

The Victim's Experience: Being Hunted

Those entangled with a psychopath often describe the experience as being hunted. They recall an uncanny sense that their vulnerabilities were mapped in advance, their defenses anticipated, their reactions studied. The psychopath's perception of others is predatory in nature —people are not seen as companions but as prey.

Survivors of psychopathic relationships frequently present with complex trauma. They exhibit hypervigilance, disorientation, self-doubt, and loss of identity. Many struggle with confusion about their own perceptions, unable to reconcile the charm they once admired with the brutality they endured. The most devastating realization is that what they mistook for intimacy was performance—an imitation of love that concealed contempt.

Clinical and Cultural Implications

Psychopathy's significance extends far beyond individual relationships. In forensic settings, psychopaths represent a disproportionate share of violent and sadistic offenders, particularly those whose crimes are planned rather than impulsive. In professional and political environments, their manipulation may never breach legality but can corrode institutions through deceit, exploitation, and moral callousness.

For mental health professionals, the implications are serious. Traditional therapeutic approaches—built on empathy, alliance, and introspection—are largely ineffective for psychopathy. Numerous studies have failed to identify any intervention that reliably alters the core traits of callousness, deceit, or manipulative dominance. Insight-oriented therapy, rather than promoting change, often refines the psychopath's ability to mimic remorse and exploit the therapist's empathy. Group therapy, intended to foster accountability, can become a training ground for manipulation. Even structured cognitive-behavioral programs yield only modest and short-lived improvements—typically in behavioral compliance, not conscience formation.

For Antisocial Personality Disorder, outcomes are somewhat more varied but remain limited. Behavioral interventions may reduce impulsivity or substance use but do not alter the personality structure that fuels exploitation. The consensus across decades of research is clear: there is no evidence-based therapy that reverses psychopathy or prevents recidivism in adults. In fact, intensive treatment of high-psychopathy offenders has occasionally produced worse outcomes, likely because it enhances social and verbal skills without increasing empathy or moral restraint.

For mental health professionals, the task is not reha-bilitation but management. Treatment, when attempted, must emphasize boundaries, external accountability, and risk containment rather than emotional transformation. Compassion without structure becomes complicity; empathy without limits becomes vulnerability.

For victims, the recommendation is more direct and more urgent. When possible, remove the psychopath or antisocial individual from your life. There is no negotia-tion, no rehabilitation through love, and no hidden good self waiting to be healed. These individuals do not change through understanding—they adapt through advantage. Where complete separation is not possible, such as co-parenting or workplace dependency, interaction must become purely transactional, minimal, and documented. Communication should be brief, factual, and preferably written. Boundaries are not cruelty—they are survival.

For society at large, psychopathy exposes the vulnerabilities of systems that reward charm, confidence, and ruthlessness. In corporate hierarchies, politics, and media, psychopathic traits often masquerade as leadership. A culture untrained in discerning charisma from conscience will repeatedly elevate predators to positions of influence. Protecting institutions therefore requires structural skepticism—oversight, accountability, and evidence-based evaluation of competence rather than charisma.

Clinically, culturally, and personally, the imperative is the same: resist the seduction of the psychopath's performance. The danger is not only in their violence but in their believability. They mimic empathy, recite remorse, and reproduce emotional language so convincingly that even experts can be drawn into their spell. Yet beneath the eloquence lies an empty architecture—cold, deliberate, and entirely self-serving.

Psychopathy and Antisocial Personality Disorder, together, represent the farthest edge of intentional cruelty. These are not individuals reacting from pain but strategizing from indifference. They charm to disarm, manipulate to dominate, and harm without remorse. Their cruelty is methodical, not defensive but offensive.

Recognizing this distinction is essential for healthcare professionals, institutions, and society to protect the innocent, hold offenders accountable, and abandon the dangerous illusion that empathy can reform the conscienceless.

To understand psychopathy is to confront the limits of compassion. The only reliable intervention is containment, and the only consistent recovery for victims begins with escape.

seven
attention as a weapon
Histrionic Personalities

AMONG CLUSTER B personality disorders, Histrionic Personality Disorder (HPD) is perhaps the most frequently trivialized. Popular portrayals often reduce it to "drama," "attention-seeking," or mere flamboyance. Yet in intimate relationships, these traits take on a coercive and manipulative dimension.

Individuals with HPD do not simply crave the spotlight; they engineer relational dynamics in which sexuality, charm, and theatricality become levers of control. The stereotype of the "life of the party" obscures the darker reality: behind the charisma, partners and friends may find themselves destabilized, discarded, or manipulated in ways that are no less damaging than the cruelty of narcissistic or psychopathic personalities.

This chapter examines the relational strategies of HPD, highlighting their manipulative elements, their superficiality, and the ways in which "drama" becomes an instrument of coercion.

Attention = Currency

At the core of HPD is an excessive need for attention and approval. Unlike narcissists, who seek admiration to confirm their superiority, individuals with HPD pursue attention as a way of feeling alive. Without it, they often describe emptiness, boredom, or despair.

Sexuality, flirtation, and exaggerated expressiveness function as tools in this pursuit. In social contexts, the histrionic individual may captivate others through bold clothing, theatrical gestures, or animated storytelling. In intimate contexts, they may deploy seduction or emotional volatility to maintain focus on themselves.

Yet the pursuit of attention is rarely benign. In relationships, attention becomes currency—a resource extracted from others through charm, coercion, or manipulation. Partners who fail to supply it are punished with sulking, flirtation with rivals, ruthless extortion, or dramatic threats of departure.

Superficiality and Fickleness

HPD is often described as shallow and flighty, a characterization that can appear dismissive until one observes its relational consequences. Individuals with HPD tend to form rapid attachments, idealizing new partners with intensity, only to discard them abruptly when novelty fades.

This cycle of pursuit and abandonment mirrors the structure of theatrical performance: a captivating act played out for a rapt audience, followed by a sudden exit when the applause wanes. To the partner left behind, the experience can feel bewildering and cruel. Affection that once seemed genuine is revealed to be contingent, existing only as long as the spotlight remained bright.

Superficiality also extends to emotional expression. The histrionic individual may appear deeply moved or passionately committed, but these displays often shift rapidly, replaced by new enthusiasms or grievances. The instability of these emotions underscores their performative quality: they are less reflections of inner states than instruments of effect.

Pathological Flirtation and Manipulative Charm

Clinical descriptions of HPD frequently emphasize pathological flirting and manipulative charm. These traits may be mistaken for mere extroversion or charisma, but in relational contexts they function as strategies of control.

The histrionic individual often uses flirtation not only to attract new partners but to destabilize existing ones. For example, a partner who fails to provide sufficient attention may be made jealous through overt displays of interest in others. This triangulation creates insecurity, compelling the partner to re-invest attention in order to "win back" the histrionic individual's favor.

Charm is equally instrumental. By captivating entire groups with theatrical energy, the histrionic person often positions themselves as indispensable or irresistible, masking the underlying instability of attachment. Those drawn into this orbit may find themselves competing for approval, a dynamic that maintains the histrionic individual's centrality.

Ruthless Extortion

One of the darker dimensions of HPD involves the extortion of attention. Histrionic individuals often demand constant attention from others, leveraging emotional displays to extract it.

Tears, dramatic threats, fainting, and outbursts may appear exaggerated or disproportionate, yet they serve a purpose: they compel others to respond, reassure, and restore the histrionic individual's sense of importance. Partners may feel as if they are held hostage to constant demands for attention.

This coercive cycle often escalates when attention shifts elsewhere. A partner's preoccupation with work, children, or even friends may be interpreted as neglect, triggering extreme reactions designed to recapture focus. Over time, the partner may feel drained, manipulated, and trapped in a relationship defined by constant performance.

Cold Abandonment

Paradoxically, while individuals with HPD can appear intensely attached, they are capable of sudden, cold abandonment. New opportunities—whether romantic, professional, or social—may take precedence over long-standing bonds. To the discarded partner, the transition feels abrupt, even shocking.

This fickleness is not merely impulsivity but reflects the underlying logic of HPD: relationships exist to serve the need for stimulation, novelty, and attention. Once a partner ceases to fulfill that function, they may be replaced with little hesitation. The emotional wreckage left behind is often rationalized as necessary or even deserved, further underscoring the manipulative character of the disorder.

Performance, Not Intimacy

The DSM-5-TR emphasizes that HPD is characterized by shallow, rapidly shifting emotions and an excessive need for attention. These features illuminate why relationships with histrionic individuals often feel like ongoing performances rather than authentic connections.

Conversations may resemble monologues, punctuated by dramatic gestures and exaggerated affect.

Conflicts may escalate into theatrical scenes, complete with accusations, sobbing, or flamboyant reconciliations. Partners may describe feeling as though they are participating in a play whose script they never agreed to.

The relational world of HPD is thus structured not by stability or reciprocity but by drama and display. Every interaction is an opportunity for performance, every relationship a stage for attention.

Clinical and Cultural Implications

Clinically, HPD presents challenges in therapy. Individuals may appear highly engaged, even charismatic in sessions, but struggle with depth, insight, or sustained change. Their fickleness often leads them to abandon therapy once they feel better, while their need for attention frequently strains therapeutic boundaries.

Culturally, HPD raises uncomfortable questions about how society rewards theatricality, beauty, and charisma. In an era of social media and curated identities, traits once confined to clinical settings and entertainment industries now play out on a global stage. The histrionic pursuit of attention may be amplified by platforms that valorize performance, creating fertile ground for these traits to flourish.

Histrionic Personality Disorder is more than flamboyance or "being dramatic." It is an enduring pattern of manipulative, attention-driven behavior that destabilizes relationships, exploits partners, and treats intimacy as performance.

From pathological flirting to cold abandonment, from extorting attention to shallow commitments, HPD reveals how the need for attention and social approval can transform into cruelty. The superficial charm of the histrionic individual conceals a deeper instability, one that leaves partners bewildered, exhausted, and discarded.

To dismiss HPD as trivial is to ignore its relational harm. Behind the curtain of performance lies a disorder that, like its Cluster B counterparts, organizes relationships around manipulation and exploitation. Recognizing this reality is essential for both clinical clarity and cultural understanding.

eight
emotional blackmail and coercion
Borderline Personalities

FEW DIAGNOSES IN mental health provoke as much debate as Borderline Personality Disorder (BPD). Among clinicians, researchers, and the public, BPD is alternately stigmatized, pathologized, romanticized, and misunderstood. The controversy arises from competing conceptualizations: some view it as an attachment-based condition, others emphasize genetic and neurobiological origins, and still others link it to Complex PTSD.

The tension in these conceptualizations is not merely academic. It shapes how patients are treated, how families interpret behavior, and how the disorder is portrayed in culture. For decades, stigma has been attached to the "borderline" label, often discouraging clinicians from even disclosing the diagnosis. Yet stigma should not obscure the reality: BPD presentations often include patterns of cruelty, retaliation, and coercive manipulation alongside profound suffering.

This chapter addresses that paradox directly. Just as denying the anguish of those afflicted is harmful, so too is ignoring the deliberate strategies of harm toward others. Both realities must be acknowledged if understanding—and effective response—are to move forward.

Between Complex PTSD and BPD

One source of confusion lies in the perceived overlap between BPD and trauma-related conditions, particularly Complex PTSD. Many individuals with BPD report histories of abandonment, neglect, or abuse, and their heightened reactivity often appears trauma-like. Yet there are legitimate reasons for differentiation.

Whereas trauma-related conditions are typically defined by avoidance, emotional numbing, and hyper-arousal, BPD is more often characterized by retaliatory behaviors, spite, and vengefulness—features absent in individuals with complex trauma. Individuals with BPD may perceive slights or abandonment without evidence, and these distortions of perception frequently result in impulsive acts of rage or violence.

The question remains whether these behaviors are primarily reactive or deliberate. Research and clinical experience indicate they are both. Many individuals with BPD, in moments of clarity, admit that their retaliatory actions are intentional as often as they are automatic. The implication is clear: cruelty in BPD cannot be dismissed as mere reactivity. It is, at times, consciously chosen.

Cruelty and Pain: A Dual Reality

The public conversation about BPD often emphasizes the pain of those who suffer: fear of abandonment, suicidal ideation, and repeated self-harm. These are real and devastating. Some individuals attempt high-risk suicides; others engage in recurrent self-mutilation. Yet alongside this reality exists another: calculated cruelty toward others.

This cruelty is not universal. BPD presents in a wide range of expressions, from "quiet" and internalized suffering to "loud" and violent externalization. The quieter presentations may be marked by depressivity, self-harm, and withdrawal. The more outwardly aggressive forms involve coercion, manipulation, betrayal, and violence.

It is often this latter group—those capable of deliberate cruelty—that is overlooked or excused. To deny the presence of cruelty in BPD is to deny reality, just as it is wrong to deny the suffering that accompanies the disorder. Both can exist simultaneously, and both must be recognized.

Cultural Portrayals: From Iconic to Infamous

Popular culture reflects the spectrum of borderline presentations. Iconic figures such as Princess Diana and Marilyn Monroe are frequently cited as public examples of individuals who may have displayed borderline traits—charismatic, emotionally turbulent, and vulnerable. In film, BPD is often sensationalized: Glenn Close's portrayal in *Fatal Attraction* and Ray Nicholson's character in *I Love You Forever* dramatize the volatile, manipulative, and retaliatory aspects of the disorder that are, in fact, true to form in many cases.

These portrayals illustrate the extremes: the sympathetic victim of inner turmoil versus the dangerous, vindictive partner. Reality is more complex. Both tenderness and cruelty can coexist in the same person, alternating rapidly and unpredictably. For those close to an individual with BPD, the experience can be one of devotion and terror, affection and hostility, intimacy and betrayal—all within a single week, day, or even hour.

Coercion Through Fear: Emotional Blackmail

In popular psychology and media, BPD is more often associated with instability and reactivity than with cold calculation. Yet abusive dynamics in borderline relationships can involve deliberate strategies of coercion. Threats of abandonment or self-harm function as powerful levers, compelling partners to remain in relationships against their better judgment.

This pattern is commonly described as emotional blackmail—a process by which the individual with BPD creates fear and obligation in others. Partners may feel responsible for the individual's very survival, terrified that leaving will precipitate suicide or self-destruction. In this way, the threat of self-harm becomes a form of control, exerting immense psychological pressure.

The paradox is clear: behaviors rooted in profound fear of abandonment can themselves drive others away, intensifying the cycle of instability and coercion.

Violence and Hostility

National survey research demonstrates that BPD is strongly associated with violence toward both self and others. Rates of suicidal behavior, self-mutilation, physical fights, and hostility are strikingly high. This dual violence—directed inward and outward—distinguishes BPD from many other conditions, including trauma-related presentations.

Emotional manipulation is often triggered by hypersensitivity to perceived rejection. When perceived slights occur, retaliation is often disproportionate—ranging from verbal attacks and threats to physical aggression. The perception itself is frequently distorted: rejection may be imagined, misinterpreted, or exaggerated. Yet the retaliation is real, leaving profound damage in its wake.

Sexual Behavior and Control

Impulsivity in BPD is not limited to aggression. Sexual behavior often functions as a form of emotional regulation or retaliation. Some individuals seek new partners when vulnerable, using seduction to reassert control or punish perceived rejection. Manipulative mate-retention tactics—such as infidelity framed as "teaching a lesson"— reflect the use of sexuality as leverage rather than intimacy.

These dynamics are frequently destructive, leaving both the individual and their partners trapped in cycles of betrayal, guilt, and retribution. These behaviors are not simply random or reactive; they are often strategic, repeated because they succeed in gaining temporary reassurance or control.

Intentionality Beneath the Chaos

Borderline aggression often appears chaotic, impulsive, and unpredictable. Yet even when emotionally charged, these behaviors serve identifiable functions: to avert imagined abandonment, reassert control, or retaliate against perceived betrayal. As Marsha Linehan's foundational work on BPD demonstrated, such strategies are not random—they are maladaptive efforts to regulate intolerable emotional states. Their recurrence across contexts suggests they are not accidents of emotional flooding but ingrained patterns.

Clinical and Cultural Implications

Understanding BPD requires holding two truths at once: individuals with the disorder are often in profound psychological pain, and many are capable of deliberate cruelty. To emphasize only one side distorts reality. Compassion without accountability risks enabling harm. Condemnation without compassion risks denying treatment to those who genuinely seek help.

Culturally, the debate over BPD reflects broader discomfort with complexity. Media tends to portray individuals with BPD either as tragic victims or as villains, rarely acknowledging that both elements can coexist. Clinically, treatment requires balancing empathy for suffering with firm boundaries against manipulation and coercion.

Ultimately, BPD must be recognized as a brain-based disorder of regulation and perception, not simply a traumatic illness or a matter of willpower. Those who are help-seeking deserve effective treatment, but the presence of suffering cannot excuse harm to others.

Cruelty is cruelty, whether reactive or intentional, and it must be named. Just as it is wrong to deny the anguish of BPD, it is wrong to deny the damage inflicted on others. Only by holding both realities—suffering and harm, vulnerability and retaliation—can we begin to respond with accuracy, accountability, and compassion.

when society excuses abuse

The Erosion of Justice

Biology and Responsibility

When we acknowledge the genetic and neurobiological roots of personality pathology, a troubling question arises: *If they were "wired this way," can we really hold abusers responsible?* Some use this reasoning to excuse or soften abusive behavior, treating it as the inevitable outcome of predisposition. But predisposition is not predestination.

Genetics provides probabilities, not certainties. A predisposition toward impulsivity or callousness does not dictate abusive action. As behavioral genetics consistently shows, heritability describes increased likelihood, not inevitability. Chronic and persistent abuse still requires choices, strategies, and deliberate actions.

Cognitive Awareness and Intentionality

Research on personality pathology reveals that disordered individuals are often cognitively aware of their actions. They can articulate the harm they cause, anticipate others' reactions, and adjust tactics to achieve their goals. Manipulative distortion of reality requires knowing another person's perception and choosing to undermine it. Isolating a partner or exploiting them requires foresight. Alternating cruelty with intermittent reward requires precision. These are not reflexive outbursts—they are intentional strategies.

The Moral Dimension of Responsibility

Moral responsibility does not require a blank slate. The law and ethics routinely hold people accountable despite predispositions and inclinations. A person with a genetic risk for aggression remains responsible for assault. A psychopath, despite neurological differences, remains responsible for calculated exploitation. To argue otherwise risks creating a world where victims are left unprotected and perpetrators are shielded by claims of biology.

Patterns of Relational Exploitation

Examining personality disorders in relational contexts clarifies accountability. Abusers across diagnostic categories display recognizable, patterned strategies designed to control, destabilize, and exploit.

Narcissistic personalities exploit others through domination and control tied to entitlement and the need for admiration. They may bully, coerce, or pursue opportunistically with little commitment, remaining hyper-attuned to others' vulnerabilities only to reinforce their superiority. Often dissatisfied in long-term partnerships, they are repulsed by genuine intimacy. For them, relationships function less as mutual bonds and more as stages for self-enhancement.

Antisocial and psychopathic personalities are defined by callousness and disregard for others' rights. Their relationships are transactional—marked by deception, coercion, reckless sexuality, and violent retaliation when thwarted. Their incapacity for love underscores a detachment from authentic intimacy.

Histrionic personalities manipulate through dramatics, seduction, and attention-seeking. Their shallow, unstable relationships hinge on novelty rather than depth. They may ruthlessly extort attention, pathologically flirt, or abandon partners once the thrill of new admiration fades. Although their methods may appear flamboyant rather than violent, their effects are destabilizing and emotionally exhausting for those involved.

Borderline personalities exploit in a more chaotic, emotionally volatile fashion. Their extreme sensitivity to perceived rejection may fuel threats of self-harm, emotional blackmail, or physical aggression. Impulsive

sexuality or abrupt mate-switching often serve as retaliation or desperate attempts to control attachment bonds.
Although such behavior may be framed as desperation or
fear, the tactics remain intentional and controlling.

The Danger of Reductive Illness Narratives

Explaining abuse as nothing more than trauma or mental
illness risks excusing perpetrators. Labeling cruelty as
"unconscious reenactment" minimizes victims' experiences, shields abusers from accountability, and undermines   prevention   by   portraying   behavior   as
uncontrollable.

For survivors of abuse, recognizing intentionality vali-
dates their experience and confirms that the cruelty they
endured was not accidental. For mental health professionals, this perspective prevents therapy from collapsing into
misplaced validation for perpetrators. For society, it
protects against myths that reframe cruelty as pain,
silencing victims in the process.

From Myth to Science

For decades, abuse has been explained through emotionally resonant but misleading narratives: the abuser as a
wounded child, an inevitable product of bad parenting,
or a casualty of trauma. These stories persist because they
offer redemption and are easier to process than the reality
of enduring traits. Yet they minimize genetic and neuro-

biological evidence and contradict survivor testimony that abuse is deliberate and patterned.

A clearer framework recognizes three interwoven influences: genetics, neurobiology, and experience. Heritable traits provide the blueprint. Brain systems regulating reward, empathy, and impulse control shape capacity for compassion or restraint. Experience in some cases may amplify or buffer predispositions, but it cannot create pathology from nothing. No specific form of trauma or adversity is either necessary or sufficient to generate severe personality pathology; predisposition remains the foundation.

At the center of this model lies a principle: *cruelty is not a symptom—it is a strategy.* Distortion of reality, isolation, coercion, and manipulation are deployed not as unconscious echoes but as deliberate choices for dominance and personal gain. Even those with strong predispositions make decisions about how, when, and against whom to deploy these tactics.

Survivors and Society at Large

For survivors, seeing abuse as strategy rather than accident restores agency and affirms perception. Cultural refrains such as *"they didn't mean it"* or *"they're just wounded"* collapse under evidence of intentionality. Validating this reality is essential for recovery.

For society, abandoning these myths is equally essential. Courts, correctional systems, and rehabilitation programs too often prioritize trauma-informed models at the expense of accountability. Acknowledging suffering may have therapeutic value, but excusing deliberate harm undermines justice. Protecting victims must take precedence over rescuing perpetrators who repeatedly choose exploitation.

Abuse is not accidental. It is a deliberate strategy— shaped by predisposition but enacted through choice. Recognizing this truth is not fatalism; it is empowerment. Moving beyond excuses is not despair but liberation. Confronting the deliberate nature of abuse prevents the silencing of survivors and the shielding of perpetrators. Aligning culture, mental healthcare, and law with scientific clarity ensures that myths no longer masquerade as compassion.

Cruelty, at its core, is a choice.

APPENDIX

appendix a.
Common Counterarguments and Clarifications

OVER THE COURSE of writing and speaking about personality disorders and abuse, I have encountered a series of recurring objections. Many of these stem from cultural narratives, clinical traditions, or misinterpretations of emerging science. They often sound persuasive at first because they echo widely repeated cultural stories or because they contain a small element of truth. Yet, when examined carefully, they fail to account for the full body of evidence.

The following sections address these counterarguments directly, showing why they may appear compelling at first glance but prove unconvincing in light of the evidence. Each theme is explored in greater depth throughout the book, with accompanying notes and empirical references provided for readers who wish to examine them further.

1. "Hurt people hurt people."

This phrase is one of the most popular cultural maxims used to explain cruelty. While it is true that trauma can create vulnerability and increase the likelihood of maladaptive coping, the evidence is clear that most abused children do not go on to become abusers themselves. Twin and sibling studies reveal striking divergence: two children raised in the same abusive household may develop in entirely different ways—one resilient and compassionate, the other callous and exploitative. Trauma is therefore best understood as a *risk factor* rather than a destiny. By suggesting a direct pipeline from victim to perpetrator, this saying risks excusing abuse and obscuring the resilience of survivors who break cycles of violence.

2. "If it's genetic, then it's destiny."

Genetics are powerful but not absolute. They establish probabilities, not certainties. Just as a family history of heart disease or diabetes increases risk without guaranteeing outcomes, genetic influences on personality traits raise the likelihood of certain patterns but leave room for variation. Heritability studies consistently demonstrate that biology matters, but outcomes emerge through *gene–environment interaction.* The fatalistic assumption that genes alone seal fate oversimplifies complex systems and can lead to despair on one hand, or misplaced fatalism about abusers on the other.

3. "They don't know what they're doing."

This is one of the most dangerous myths because it strips abusers of agency. In reality, many individuals who engage in abuse employ highly deliberate and recognizable tactics: truth manipulation, triangulation, charm campaigns, calculated impression management, and targeted devaluation. These behaviors require forethought and strategy. Lack of empathy is not the same as lack of awareness. Indeed, the effectiveness of these tactics often depends on the abuser's keen ability to read social cues and exploit them. To imagine abuse as a mindless or unconscious act is to misunderstand the calculated nature of manipulation.

4. "But what about epigenetics? Doesn't trauma switch genes on and off?"

Epigenetics is often misunderstood as a mechanism that makes trauma the root cause of pathology. In fact, epigenetics highlights the interaction between genes and environment, not the dominance of one over the other. While trauma can influence how certain genes are expressed, it cannot manufacture traits that are not already biologically possible. Epigenetics enriches our understanding by showing how predispositions are shaped in context, but it does not support the idea that environment alone "creates" personality disorders. The findings reinforce heritability rather than overturn it.

5. "Cluster B personalities act out of shame."

Shame is part of the human condition, but it is not a defining feature of Cluster B personality disorders. Some individuals with these disorders may experience shame, while others appear largely immune to it. What defines Cluster B pathology are enduring traits such as entitlement, callousness, dominance-seeking, emotional volatility, and lack of empathy. These traits drive cruelty, exploitation, manipulation, and coercion far more reliably than fluctuating feelings of shame. Reducing Cluster B pathology to a shame-based model obscures the stable, dispositional qualities that actually predict harmful and abusive behavior.

6. "They abuse because they were abused."

While trauma may influence development, it does not dictate outcomes. Many survivors of horrific abuse live lives marked by compassion and a commitment never to repeat the harm they endured. To claim that all abusers were once victims not only insults resilient survivors but also hands abusers an easy narrative with which to justify or excuse their behavior. The reality is that abuse is often strategic and chosen, and abusers sometimes exploit their trauma histories as tools of manipulation. Acknowledging trauma does not erase responsibility.

7. "They are just more sensitive than others."

This explanation confuses vulnerability with predation. Sensitivity can indeed make a person more susceptible to anxiety, depression, or relational difficulties, but it does not explain the deliberate cruelty and exploitation that characterize personality pathology. In fact, many individuals with callous–unemotional traits appear less sensitive to stress, less vulnerable to guilt, and more resistant to empathy. These traits often make abusers more, not less, capable of sustaining harmful behaviors without internal conflict.

8. "If it's a disorder, doesn't that mean they aren't responsible?"

Medicalized language can unintentionally blur lines of accountability. A diagnosis describes a pattern of traits and behaviors; it does not erase the capacity for choice. Personality pathology influences tendencies and inclinations, but individuals remain responsible for how they act on those tendencies. Just as having a predisposition toward aggression does not absolve assault, having a personality disorder does not nullify responsibility for deliberate abuse. Confusing explanation with excuse undermines both justice and clinical clarity.

9. "But can't people change?"

Change is possible but rare and difficult. Personality pathology is deeply ingrained, taking root in childhood and persisting across the lifespan. While some individuals may learn to manage or soften specific behaviors, the prognosis for fundamental transformation is often poor. Therapeutic gains are more often about containment and harm reduction than about total change of character. It is far safer—and more accurate—to evaluate abusers by their established behavioral patterns rather than invest in hypothetical potential for change.

10. "Isn't everyone a little narcissistic?"

It is true that narcissistic traits exist on a spectrum, and nearly everyone displays self-interest or vanity at times. But this does not equate to narcissistic personality disorder or to the deliberate cruelty associated with pathological narcissism. Casual overuse of the term dilutes its meaning and obscures the difference between everyday self-focus and entrenched exploitative behavior. Recognizing this distinction is critical for clarity in both clinical practice and survivor advocacy.

11. "They just need more love."

This romanticized view assumes that pathology can be corrected by patience, devotion, or sacrifice. While loving relationships can be protective factors for many forms of human suffering, the entrenched traits of personality disorders are not cured by affection. Survivors who are persuaded to "love harder" often end up trapped in cycles of exploitation, believing they are failing when in reality the pathology lies in the abuser's enduring disposition. Love cannot undo callousness, entitlement, or lack of empathy.

12. "Maybe they don't mean it."

Minimization of abuse is another common defense. Yet the repetition, calculation, and consistency of abusive behaviors speak otherwise. Even if an abuser occasionally lashes out impulsively, patterns of coercion, manipulation, and exploitation over time reveal intent. To dismiss abuse as accidental is to ignore the weight of evidence survivors bring: that these acts are not random but deliberate.

Final Note

Counterarguments against intentional cruelty endure because they contain a grain of truth. But as explanations for abuse, they explain less than they obscure. Abuse is not simply a reflexive response to pain, nor the deterministic product of trauma, nor merely an exaggeration of ordinary human flaws. The evidence is clear: abuse is often a *strategy*—chosen, repeated, and reinforced—by individuals whose genetic and neurobiological makeup predisposes them toward manipulation, exploitation, and control.

This appendix provides a concise overview, but readers are encouraged to consult the relevant chapters of this book, where these arguments are examined in detail and supported with scholarly references.

appendix b.

Cruelty Assessment: A Gut Check on Character

THE FOLLOWING ASSESSMENT is not meant to diagnose or label anyone, nor is it designed to reduce people to categories. Instead, it is a tool to help you reflect on patterns of behavior you may encounter in others. Survivors of abuse often struggle with second-guessing their perceptions or rationalizing cruelty. These questions are meant to give language to behaviors that corrode trust, destabilize relationships, and signal patterns of manipulation or control.

Use this as a mirror for the people in your life—past or present. Recognizing cruelty is not about judgment; it is about protection. By naming behaviors clearly, you affirm your perceptions and give yourself permission to set boundaries. This tool is designed to help you identify extremes so you can make choices that safeguard your well-being and restore a sense of safety and self-trust.

How to Use This Assessment

For each question, think of the person you are reflecting on and choose the response that fits best:

- *Not really them*

- *Sometimes them*

- *Often Them*

THERE ARE NO RIGHT OR WRONG ANSWERS. The value lies in noticing patterns over time.

Prejudice & Bias

- They make assumptions about people based on race, gender, or appearance.
- They laugh at or share jokes that stereotype others.
- They suggest that some groups of people are less valuable than others.
- They dismiss someone's viewpoint because of background or identity.
- They hold resentment toward people who are different from them.

Power & Control

- They use sarcasm or put-downs to win arguments.
- They manipulate situations to get their way, even if it disadvantages others.
- They enjoy seeing others lose if it benefits them.
- They become hostile or aggressive when they feel slighted.
- They believe rules don't always apply to them.

Relationships & Empathy

- They withdraw affection, attention, or support as a way to punish.
- They pressure others into doing things they don't want to do.
- They treat people better when those people can offer something in return.
- They ignore the needs of others when those needs are inconvenient.
- They rarely stop to consider how their words or actions affect others.

Indifference & Exploitation

- They show little guilt when they hurt someone emotionally.
- They take advantage of others if they think they won't get caught.
- They gossip or spread rumors for entertainment or advantage.
- They disregard others' boundaries when those boundaries conflict with their desires.
- They view people more as obstacles or tools than as human beings.

Integrity & Character

- They downplay or excuse harmful behavior rather than take responsibility.
- They take credit for things they didn't do.
- They cut corners or cheat if it gives them an edge.
- They value winning or looking good more than fairness.
- They believe cruelty can be justified if it helps them succeed.

Reflection Guide

- *"Not really them"* → This person generally treats others with empathy and respect. Keep observing, but the overall pattern suggests integrity.
- *"Sometimes them"* → Pay attention. These behaviors can harm over time, even if they don't happen constantly. Consider whether the relationship feels safe and balanced.
- *"Often them"* → This is a red flag. Patterns of cruelty and manipulation are consistent, not occasional. Take seriously how these behaviors affect your safety, dignity, and well-being.

Closing Note

As you reflect on your answers, remember: cruelty is not an accident. If these patterns show up repeatedly in someone's behavior, they are strategies — not slips. Your instincts matter. If you see cruelty clearly, you are not imagining it or being too sensitive.

We all share the same human DNA, shaped in a world where suspicion, dominance, and aggression once helped us survive. But what may have served ancient survival harms modern relationships when taken to extremes. Recognizing cruelty for what it is allows you to protect yourself and choose relationships that are rooted in respect, trust, and care.

appendix c.
The Social Predator's Cruelty Playbook

THROUGHOUT THIS BOOK, we've examined how cultural narratives often obscure the deliberate nature of cruelty. This section moves from theory to practice—a field guide to the social predator's playbook. The following tactics reveal that manipulation is not a reflex of pain but a calculated strategy: a series of deliberate maneuvers designed to confuse, control, and consume. Recognizing these patterns restores clarity to those who have been targeted and dismantles the illusion that cruelty stems merely from emotional suffering or misunderstanding.

Deceptive Communication

- **Overt Lies** – Plain, intentional falsehoods used to rewrite reality. The deceiver denies what is obvious, forcing the partner to question their own perception.

- **Lies of Omission** – Strategic silence: withholding critical information to manipulate outcomes while maintaining plausible innocence.
- **Playing Dumb** – Feigned confusion or selective memory to avoid responsibility. The abuser pretends ignorance to stall accountability and wear the victim down.
- **Lies with Truth Mixed In** – Partial honesty blended with distortion. By including a factual detail, the manipulator gives their deception credibility.
- **Rapid-Fire Speech** – Overwhelming the listener with a barrage of words and justifications until clarity collapses and the victim concedes out of fatigue.
- **White Lies** – Small, dismissive deceptions that signal disregard for the victim's awareness and normalize dishonesty in daily interaction.
- **Feigning Fear** – Pretending vulnerability to shift blame: the manipulator claims fear of the victim's reaction to excuse concealment or deceit.
- **Manufactured Vulnerability** – Dramatic self-disclosure or exaggerated confessions

meant to evoke sympathy and deflect scrutiny, not to express truth.

- **Malingering and Excuses** – Fabricating illness, fatigue, or emotional fragility to avoid duties, intimacy, or confrontation.
- **Self-Victimization and Pity Plays** – Framing oneself as the wounded party to trigger guilt and secure compliance or resources.
- **Lying About Lying** – Moral posturing: emphatic declarations of honesty designed to mask chronic deception.
- **Withdrawal Lies** – Feigned unavailability, reversed sleep schedules, or selective absence to create distance and reassert control.
- **Strategic Vagueness** – Offering ambiguous answers or noncommittal statements to evade accountability while appearing cooperative.
- **False Equivalence** – Equating minor mistakes by the victim with major acts of harm by the predator to blur moral and factual distinctions.
- **Information Flooding** – Providing excessive, irrelevant detail to obscure deception or derail a discussion.
- **Intentional Misinterpretation** – Twisting another's words to create conflict or justify retaliation.

Manipulation Tactics: The Idealization Phase

- **Seduction** – Excessive affection, flattery, and attention that mimic intimacy but serve to disarm judgment and accelerate attachment.
- **Volunteering Virtue** – Announcing moral purity or honesty before it is questioned to preempt suspicion and gain premature trust.
- **Unanticipated Self-Disclosure** – Sharing personal or tragic stories early to appear vulnerable and trustworthy, prompting reciprocal confessions they can later weaponize.
- **Lip Service** – Making sweeping promises or declarations of devotion that will never align with behavior, used to maintain control through words rather than consistency.
- **Self-Pity** – Recasting themselves as a misunderstood or mistreated soul to appeal to empathy and lower defenses.
- **Shifting Tone of Voice** – Using calculated changes in vocal tone—softer, childlike, trembling—to trigger protectiveness or guilt.
- **Triangulation (Phase I)** – Inserting a third person into the dynamic—real or imagined—to evoke jealousy, insecurity, or competition, reinforcing the predator's power.

- **Mirroring and Persona Crafting** –
  Imitating the victim's values, humor, and
  interests to fabricate compatibility.
- **False Future Planning** – Fantasizing shared
  futures (travel, marriage, collaboration) to
  deepen investment and distract from early
  warning signs.
- **Enlisting Allies** – Charming the victim's
  friends, family, or colleagues to build external
  credibility and isolate the target.

Manipulation Tactics: The Devaluation Phase

- **Intermittent Reinforcement** – Alternating
  affection and rejection to condition the
  victim to seek approval, creating emotional
  dependency.
- **Triangulation (Phase II)** – Comparing the
  victim unfavorably to others or rekindling
  contact with new admirers to provoke self-
  doubt.
- **Reality Distortion** – A systematic
  manipulation of facts and perceptions
  designed to make the victim doubt their own
  memory, judgment, and sanity—creating
  confusion that ensures compliance and
  control.

- **Crying on Demand** – Performing distress or remorse to reset emotional tone and regain control when exposed or confronted.
- **Criticism, Contempt, and Mockery** – Replacing admiration with ridicule, sarcasm, or moral superiority to erode confidence.
- **Invalidation** – Dismissing or trivializing feelings to suggest that emotional reactions are irrational or manipulative.
- **Withholding Affection** – Using physical or emotional distance as punishment or leverage.
- **Covert Admissions of Guilt** – Confessions disguised as concern—projecting their own wrongdoing onto the victim.
- **Blame-Shifting** – Attributing their own motives or actions to the victim, forcing them to defend against false accusations.
- **Word Salad and Diversion** – Rambling, irrelevant, or circular dialogue meant to derail clarity and maintain dominance in conversation.
- **Minimization and Rationalization** – Reinterpreting harm as exaggeration, misunderstanding, or mutual fault.
- **Feigning Altruism or Innocence** – Pretending to act in the victim's best interest or claiming naivety to mask calculated manipulation.

- **Guilt-Tripping and Shaming** – Exploiting empathy to make the victim responsible for the predator's moods, failures, or cruelty.

- **Manufactured Anger** – Controlled outbursts turned on and off at will to intimidate and regain compliance.

- **Public Reversal** – Praising the victim in private but criticizing or mocking them publicly.

- **Private Reversal** – Complimenting or admiring the victim publicly while demeaning, devaluing, or ridiculing them in private. The abuser uses public charm to build an image of affection and respect, then reverses it behind closed doors to assert dominance and control. This duality isolates the victim—others see apparent kindness while the victim experiences cruelty that no one else witnesses.

- **Selective Generosity** – Offering favors or apologies after cruelty to confuse moral evaluation and keep the victim hopeful.

- **Performative Contrition** – Visible displays of guilt or sadness for an audience rather than for repair.

- **Preemptive Narrative Control** – Telling others their version of events before the victim can speak.

Manipulation Tactics: The Abandonment Phase

- **Stonewalling** – Withdrawing communication or affection completely to punish, confuse, or force pursuit.
- **Re-Engagement** – Attempts to draw the victim back through apologies, nostalgia, or fabricated crises once the predator feels their control fading.
- **Feigning Regret or Remorse** – Expressions of sorrow designed to reinitiate contact or maintain moral leverage, not to repair harm.
- **False Concessions** – Pretending to agree or change while secretly maintaining the same behavior.
- **Giving Assent** – Offering surface-level compliance or agreement purely to silence confrontation and escape accountability.
- **Token Closure** – Offering a staged final conversation or written apology to appear mature while reopening emotional wounds.
- **Smear Campaigns** – Recruiting others to spread half-truths and character attacks after discard.
- **Proxy Contact** – Using mutual acquaintances or online intermediaries to deliver messages or monitor the victim.

Closing Note

The cruelty of social predators lies not in isolated acts but in orchestration. Each tactic—flattery, deceit, pity, rage—is a deliberate move in a psychological design intended to dominate perception and dismantle autonomy. Recognizing these maneuvers restores power to the deceived, clarity to the confused, and justice to those who have been made to doubt their own reality. Awareness is not cynicism—it is protection; and knowledge of the playbook is the beginning of freedom.

appendix d.
Traits That Make A Dangerous Mate

A PERSONALITY TRAIT is a consistent tendency to think, feel, perceive, believe, and behave in particular ways across time and circumstance. Unlike symptoms, which fluctuate with stress, environment, or mood, traits are enduring features of one's character. They are biologically based and, like physical traits, heritable—not learned habits or temporary reactions to life events.

The following traits represent patterns commonly found in individuals with disordered or high-conflict personalities. You may recognize some of these in relationships where manipulation, volatility, or emotional harm were persistent themes.

Emotional Lability

Marked instability of mood and emotion; heightened

reactivity; rapid, intense, and unpredictable mood swings that are disproportionate to circumstances.

Hostility

Chronic irritability and contempt; frequent anger or rage in response to minor frustrations; a tendency toward cruelty, vindictiveness, and spiteful retaliation.

Perseveration

Rigid repetition of ineffective behaviors or strategies despite clear evidence of negative consequences; inability or refusal to adapt once a pattern has been established.

Antagonism

A deliberate oppositional stance toward others; fostering conflict to assert control; domineering, self-serving, and vindictive in interpersonal style.

Manipulativeness

Skillful use of deceit, charm, or coercion to influence and exploit others; employing emotional appeals or calculated subterfuge to achieve self-focused goals; presenting a false or seductive façade to conceal true motives.

Deceitfulness

Habitual distortion or fabrication of facts; constructing misleading narratives or false impressions; chronic dishonesty and moral duplicity in communication and behavior.

Dominance

A compulsive need for control and authority; assertive to the point of coercion; dismissive of collaboration or differing viewpoints.

Grandiosity

Arrogance and entitlement; belief in one's superiority or special status; inflated self-importance coupled with disdain for others' opinions or needs.

Attention Seeking

A persistent craving for admiration and visibility; engaging in dramatization or crisis creation to remain the center of focus; equating attention with self-worth.

Callousness

Cold indifference to others' rights and feelings; lack of

empathy, guilt, or remorse for harm caused; deriving satis-
faction from dominance or others' distress.

Exhibitionism

An exaggerated, theatrical display of emotion or behavior
intended to captivate attention; often expressed through
provocative, flamboyant, or sensational presentation.

Rudeness

Interpersonal insensitivity marked by bluntness, tactless-
ness, and disregard for social boundaries or emotional
impact.

Social Norm Violation

Persistent disregard for societal rules, ethics, or laws; defi-
ance of authority; antisocial or rebellious behavior
presented as self-justified autonomy.

Gratification Seeking

Orientation toward immediate pleasure or reward; impulsive pursuit of desire without reflection on consequences
or consideration of others' needs.

Irresponsibility

Disregard for obligations, commitments, or promises; chronic failure to honor agreements or meet responsibilities; absence of reliability and follow-through.

Impulsivity

Acting on urges or emotions without forethought or concern for outcome; difficulty pausing, planning, or anticipating negative consequences.

Risk Taking

Seeking stimulation through dangerous or reckless activity; thrill-driven disregard for personal limits or potential harm; equating risk with vitality or superiority.

Restricted Affect

Limited or blunted emotional range; subdued or detached response to emotional situations; indifference or discomfort in expressions of empathy, joy, or connection.

A Final Word of Caution

While everyone occasionally acts of character under heightened stress, an enduring and pervasive pattern of pathological trait expression signals profound disturbance. These characteristics erode safety, trust, and reciprocity over time.

If you recognize multiple traits in someone close to you, consider it a **warning sign**, not a challenge to fix or understand. Dangerous personalities do not heal through empathy—they exploit it. Awareness is protection. Boundaries, distance, and support from informed professionals or trusted allies are essential safeguards against being drawn into a cycle of harm disguised as love.

references

American Psychiatric Association. (2022). *Diagnostic and statistical manual of mental disorders (5th ed., text rev.)* (5th ed.). American Psychiatric Association.

- Refined diagnostic descriptions and clarified overlaps among narcissistic, antisocial, borderline, and histrionic features. The text revision enhances differential-diagnosis precision and improves consistency across research and clinical applications.

Ash, S., Greenwood, D., & Keenan, J. P. (2023). The neural correlates of narcissism: Is there a connection with desire for fame and celebrity worship? *Brain Science, 13.* https://doi.org/10.3390/brain sci13101499

- Explores the neural correlates of narcissism with a focus on its association with fame-seeking and celebrity worship behaviors. Using neuroimaging and personality measures, the authors identify overlapping activation patterns in brain regions linked to self-referential processing, reward anticipation, and social comparison, including the medial prefrontal cortex and striatum. The study supports the view that narcissism is neurobiologically tied to reward-based motivation for recognition and status, bridging personality neuroscience with contemporary cultural expressions of narcissistic desire.

Atkinson, J. R., Kristinsdottir, K. H., Lee, T., & Freestone, M. C. (2024). Comparing the symptom presentation similarities and differences of complex posttraumatic stress disorder and borderline personality disorder: A systematic review. *Personality disorders: Theory, research, and treatment, 15*(4), 241-253.

- Conducted a systematic review comparing the symptom profiles of complex posttraumatic stress disorder (C-PTSD) and borderline personality disorder (BPD). The review found substantial overlap in affective instability, interpersonal difficulties, and self-concept disturbances but noted key distinctions—particularly the role of trauma-related intrusions, hyperarousal, and avoidance in C-PTSD versus pervasive identity disturbance, retaliatory aggression, and hostility in BPD. The study clarifies the diagnostic overlap and separation between the two conditions, emphasizing that these differing emotional and behavioral mechanisms refine clinical case formulation and support more accurate differential diagnosis.

Babiak, P., & Hare, R. D. (2019). *Snakes in Suits: Understanding and surviving the psychopaths in your office* (Rev. ed.). Harper.

- Examines how individuals with psychopathic traits manipulate organizational structures for personal gain. Drawing from clinical research and real-world case studies, the authors describe the charm, deceit, and strategic aggression that enable psychopaths to ascend in professional settings. The revised edition integrates new findings on psychopathy's neurobiological and behavioral underpinnings, offering practical guidance for recognizing and mitigating the destructive impact of manipulative personalities in the workplace.

Baker, L. A. (2007). The biology of relationships: What behavioral genetics tells us about interactions among family members. *De Paul Law Review, 56*(3), 837-846.

- Reviews findings from behavioral genetics to explain how genetic factors shape family interactions and relationship dynamics. Emphasizes that traits influencing parenting, sibling relationships, and marital functioning are themselves heritable, challenging the assumption that family environments operate independently of biology. The article highlights gene–environment correlation as a key mechanism through which genetic predispositions influence both the formation and quality of interpersonal relationships within families.

Bartz, J. A., Simeon, D., Hamilton, H., Kim, S., Crystal, S., Braun, A., Vicens, V., & Hollander, E. (2011). Oxytocin can hinder trust and cooperation in borderline personality disorder. *Social Cognitive and Affective Neuroscience, 6*(5), 556–563.

- Demonstrates that intranasal oxytocin can paradoxically heighten mistrust and defensive responses in individuals with BPD, challenging its popular characterization as a universal "bonding hormone." The findings underscore the context-dependent and person-specific nature of oxytocin's influence on social cognition and attachment processes in personality pathology.

Beam, C. R., Pezzoli, P., Mendle, J., Burt, S. A., Neale, M. C., Boker, S. M., Keel, P. K., & Klump, K. L. (2022). How nonshared environmental factors come to correlate with heredity. *Developmental Psychopathology, 34*(1), 321-333.

- Investigates how nonshared environmental factors—experiences unique to individuals within the same family—can become correlated with genetic influences over time. Using longitudinal twin data, the study demonstrates that genetic predispositions can shape individuals' exposure to distinct environmental contexts, leading to dynamic gene–environment correlations. The

findings refine developmental psychopathology models
by illustrating how heritable traits actively influence
environmental selection and experience, blurring the false
boundary between "nature" and "nurture."

Belsky, J., & Pluess, M. (2009). The nature (and nurture?) of plasticity
in early human development. *Perspectives on Psychological Science,
4*(4), 345–351. https://doi.org/10.1111/j.1745-6924.2009.01136.x

- Shows that certain genotypes confer heightened plasticity
  —leading to either resilience or risk depending on
  context. Reframes "vulnerability" as environmental
  sensitivity, supporting the gene–environment interaction
  model central to modern personality research.

Blair, J. R., Mitchell, D. G. V., & Blair, K. S. (2005). *The psychopath:
Emotion and the brain.* Blackwell Publishing.

- Examines amygdala and orbitofrontal cortex dysfunction
  underlying moral learning and affective empathy deficits
  in psychopathy. Provides a neurocognitive model
  explaining how psychopathic individuals may
  intellectually simulate remorse and empathy without
  genuine affective experience.

Bornovalova, M. A., Hicks, B. M., Iacono, W. G., & McGue, M. (2009).
Stability, change, and heritability of borderline personality disorder
traits from adolescence to adulthood: A longitudinal twin study.
Development and Psychopathology, 21(4), 1335-1353.

- Longitudinal twin study to examine the stability, change,
  and heritability of borderline personality disorder (BPD)
  traits from adolescence into adulthood. Their analyses
  revealed that BPD traits show moderate to high
  heritability (approximately 40–60%) and remain
  relatively stable over time, with genetic factors

accounting for much of this continuity. The findings indicate that while environmental influences contribute to short-term fluctuations, enduring genetic liability underlies the persistent emotional dysregulation and impulsivity characteristic of BPD.

Bornovalova, M. A., Verhulst, B., Webber, T., McGue, M., Iacono, W. G., & Hicks, B. M. (2018). Genetic and environmental influences on the co-development between borderline personality disorder traits, major depression symptoms, and substance use disorder symptoms from adolescence to young adulthood. *Development and Psychopathology,* *30*(1), 49–65. https://doi.org/10.1017/S0954579417000463

- Used longitudinal twin data to examine how genetic and environmental factors contribute to the co-development of borderline personality disorder (BPD) traits, depression, and substance use across adolescence and young adulthood. The study found that shared genetic influences largely explain the overlap among these conditions, particularly traits related to impulsivity and emotional dysregulation. These findings underscore early temperament and heritable vulnerability as central drivers of BPD's developmental trajectory, challenging trauma-exclusive models of its etiology.

Bornstein, R. F., Denckla, C. A., & Chung, W.-J. (2015). Dependent and histrionic personality disorders. In P. H. Blaney, R. F. Krueger, & T. Millon (Eds.), *Oxford textbook of psychopathology* (3rd ed., pp. 659–680). Oxford University Press.

- Provides an in-depth overview of dependent and histrionic personality disorders within Millon's integrative biopsychosocial framework. The chapter reviews diagnostic criteria, developmental pathways, and empirical findings, highlighting how dependency and emotional expressiveness emerge from both dispositional and interpersonal factors. The authors emphasize differential diagnosis, comorbidity patterns, and evidence-based treatment strategies, situating these disorders along continua of attachment, self-concept, and social reinforcement.

Brummelman, E., Gurel, C., Thomaes, S., & Sedikides, C. (2018). What separates narcissism from self-esteem? A social-cognitive perspective. In Anthony D. Hermann, Amy B. Brunell, & Joshua D. Foster (Eds.), *Handbook of trait narcissism: Key advances, research methods, and controversies* (pp. 47-55). Springer International Publishing.

- Differentiates narcissism from healthy self-esteem through mechanisms of self-enhancement and contingent validation. Argues that narcissism relies on external affirmation and dominance motives, whereas self-esteem reflects autonomous, stable self-regard—clarifying a crucial diagnostic and developmental distinction.

Buss, D. M. (2025). *Evolutionary psychology: The new science of the mind* (7th ed.). Routledge.

- Presents a comprehensive synthesis of evolutionary psychology, exploring how natural and sexual selection have shaped human cognition, emotion, and behavior. The text integrates findings from genetics, neuroscience, and cross-cultural research to explain adaptive strategies underlying traits such as aggression, mate selection, and social competition. By framing personality and psychopathology as evolutionary variants of adaptive mechanisms, the text provides a foundational perspective for understanding the biological and functional origins of complex social behaviors.

Carter, C. S. (2014). *Oxytocin pathways and the evolution of human behavior. Annual Review of Psychology, 65*, 17–39. https://doi.org/10.1146/annurev-psych-010213-115110

- Reviews the neuroendocrine pathways of oxytocin, showing that the hormone can facilitate trust, bonding, or strategic manipulation depending on social context. Emphasizes that oxytocin's effects are motivationally opportunistic rather than inherently prosocial, offering a nuanced, evolutionary perspective on affiliative behavior.

Craig, M. C., Catani, M., Deeley, Q., Latham, R., Daly, E., Kanaan, R., ... Murphy, D. G. M. (2009). Altered connections on the road to psychopathy. *Molecular Psychiatry, 14*(10), 946–953.

- Identifies reduced integrity of the uncinate fasciculus linking the amygdala and ventromedial prefrontal cortex in psychopathy. Provides structural evidence for disrupted emotional regulation and moral reasoning, explaining instrumental cruelty through neural network dysfunction.

DiLalla, F. L., Diaz, E., & Jamnik, M. R. (2020). Toward the dark side: Temperament, personality, and genetics related to antisocial behaviors. In K.J. Saudino and J.M. Ganiban (Ed.), *Behavior genetics of temperament and personality* (pp. 193-213). Springer International .

- Explores how genetic and temperamental predispositions contribute to the development of antisocial and aggressive behaviors. Integrating behavioral genetic research with developmental models, the authors identify early-emerging traits such as low agreeableness, impulsivity, and callous-unemotional tendencies as key risk factors. The chapter underscores the heritable foundations of antisociality while acknowledging environmental moderators, offering a nuanced view of how temperament and personality interact in the emergence of externalizing pathology.

Di Sarno, M., Di Pierro, R., & Madeddu, F. (2018). The relevance of neuroscience for the investigation of narcissism: A review of current studies [Abstract]. *Clinical Neuropsychiatry, 15*(4), 242.

- Reviews neuroscientific research examining structural and functional brain correlates of narcissism. Highlights consistent findings of altered activity in regions associated with empathy, self-referential processing, and reward sensitivity, including the anterior insula and prefrontal cortex. Emphasizes that integrating neuroscience with psychodynamic and clinical approaches enhances understanding of narcissism's cognitive–affective mechanisms and its distinction from other personality pathologies.

Distel, M. A., Trull, T. J., Willemsen, G., Vink, J. M., Derom, C. A., Lynskey, M., Martin, N. G., & Boomsma, D. I. (2009). The five-factor model of personality and borderline personality disorder: A genetic analysis of comorbidity. *Biological Psychiatry, 66*1131-1138.

- Used a large twin sample to examine the genetic overlap between borderline personality disorder (BPD) traits and the Five-Factor Model (FFM) of personality. The results revealed substantial genetic correlations between BPD and high neuroticism, as well as inverse associations with agreeableness and conscientiousness. The study demonstrates that shared genetic influences account for much of the comorbidity between normal personality variation and borderline pathology, supporting dimensional and heritable models of personality disorders.

Dowgwillo, E. A., & Pincus, A. L. (2017). Differentiating Dark Triad traits within and across interpersonal circumplex surfaces. *Assessment, 24*(1), 24–44. https://doi.org/10.1177/1073191116643161

- This study uses the interpersonal circumplex model to map narcissism, Machiavellianism, and psychopathy onto distinct interpersonal trait profiles. The study demonstrates that while all three traits share antagonistic core features, they diverge in dominance, warmth, and exploitative interpersonal strategies. The findings clarify structural overlaps and distinctions among Dark Triad constructs, supporting more precise personality assessment and theoretical differentiation.

Fan, Y., Wonneberger, C., Enzi, B., de Greck, M., Ulrich, C., Tempelmann, C., Bogerts, B., Doering, S., & Northoff, G. (2011). The narcissistic self and its psychological and neural correlates: An exploratory fMRI study. *Psychological Medicine, 41*(8), 1641–1650. https://doi.org/10.1017/S003329171000228X

- This fMRI study explores how narcissistic personality traits are reflected in brain activity during self-referential processing. The findings suggest that narcissism involves heightened neural engagement with self-related information, linking the psychological construct of grandiosity to specific neural mechanisms of self-focus and affective control.

Fanti, K. A., & Frangou, G. (2018). Narcissism and Bullying. In A.D. Hermann, A.B. Brunell, & J.D. Foster (Eds.), *Handbook of trait narcissism: Key advances, research methods, and controversies* (pp. 455-470). Springer International Publishing.

- Examines the intersection of narcissism and bullying across development, identifying grandiose narcissism as a driver of proactive aggression and dominance-seeking. Emphasizes that narcissistic bullying reflects calculated self-enhancement rather than impulsive hostility, mediated by callous-unemotional traits and poor affect regulation.

Farde, L., Plaven-Sigray, P., Borg, J., & Cervenka, S. (2018). Brain neuroreceptor density and personality traits: Towards dimensional biomarkers for psychiatric disorders. *Philosophical Transactions Royal Society London B* , *373*(1744), . https://doi.org/0.1098/rstb. 2017.0156

- Reviews neuroimaging studies linking neurotransmitter receptor densities—particularly dopaminergic and serotonergic systems—to personality dimensions such as impulsivity, harm avoidance, and reward dependence. The review argues that variability in receptor availability may serve as a biological substrate for stable personality traits, bridging neurochemistry and behavioral genetics. The authors propose that such biomarkers could inform dimensional approaches to psychiatric diagnosis by mapping neurobiological correlates across normal and disordered personality continua.

Fearon, P., Shmueli-Goetz, Y., Viding, E., Fonagy, P., & Plomin, R. (2014). Genetic and environmental influences on adolescent attachment. *Journal of Child Psychology & Psychiatry., 55*(9), 1033-1041.

- Used twin data to disentangle genetic and environmental contributions to adolescent attachment security. Their findings revealed that attachment patterns show moderate heritability, with genetic factors explaining roughly one-third of the variance, while shared environmental effects were minimal. The study challenges purely environmental models of attachment, demonstrating that individual differences in attachment behavior partly reflect heritable temperament and emotion-regulation mechanisms.

Foster, J. D., & Brunell, A. B. (2018). Narcissism and Romantic Relationships. In A.D. Hermann, A.B. Brunell, & J.D. Foster (Eds.), *Handbook of trait narcissism: Key advances, research methods, and controversies* (pp. 317-326). Springer.

- Synthesizes research linking narcissistic traits to idealization–devaluation cycles, infidelity, and relational exploitation. Shows how narcissism undermines empathy, commitment, and mutuality, providing a framework for understanding relational abuse and manipulation in intimate partnerships.

Friedel, R. O., Schmahl, C., & Distel, M. (2018). The neurobiological basis of borderline personality disorder. In C. Schmahl, K.L. Phan, R.O. Friedel, & L.J. Siever (Eds.), *Neurobiology of personality disorders* (pp. 279-317). Oxford University Press.

- Reviews fronto-limbic dysregulation, serotonergic imbalance, and threat-sensitivity mechanisms underlying BPD. Emphasizes emotion-regulation-first treatment targets such as dialectical-behavioral strategies and pharmacologic modulation of affective instability.

Gagne, J. R., & Goldsmith, H. H. (2020). Development of temperament in infancy and childhood. In K.J. Saudino & J. M. Ganiban (Eds.), *Behavior genetics of temperament and personality* (pp. 3-30). Springer.

- Reviews the genetic and developmental foundations of temperament from infancy through early childhood. Drawing on twin and longitudinal studies, the review demonstrates that core temperamental traits—such as emotional reactivity, effortful control, and sociability— are moderately heritable and stable over time. The chapter highlights gene–environment interplay and early self-regulation as critical processes linking biological temperament to later personality development and psychopathology risk.

George, F. R., & Short, D. (2017). The cognitive neuroscience of narcissism. *Science Publications,* 1-14.

- Synthesize emerging research on the neural and cognitive mechanisms underlying narcissism. Discusses how abnormalities in self-referential processing, reward sensitivity, and empathy networks—particularly within the prefrontal cortex, anterior insula, and default mode network—contribute to narcissistic traits. The paper integrates findings from neuroscience and psychology to propose a multidimensional model linking narcissism's cognitive distortions and emotional dysregulation to identifiable neural systems.

Gu, X., Gao, Z., Wang, X., Liu, X., Knight, R. T., Hof, P. R., & Fan, J. (2012). Anterior insular cortex is necessary for empathetic pain perception. *Brain , 135*(9), 2726-35.

- Used lesion and functional imaging methods to investigate the role of the anterior insula in empathy for pain. The study demonstrated that damage to this region abolishes the ability to experience empathetic pain responses, confirming its essential role in affective resonance and interoceptive awareness. These findings establish the anterior insula as a key neural hub for emotional empathy, with implications for understanding deficits observed in psychopathy and narcissistic personality disorder.

Hare, R. D. (1993). *Without conscience: The disturbing world of the psychopaths among us.* The Guilford Press.

- Introduces the Psychopathy Checklist–Revised (PCL-R) and delineates core affective and interpersonal deficits—callousness, deceit, and shallow affect. Remains the seminal text explaining why remorse displays are often strategic rather than reparative.

Hare, R. D. (2003). *Hare PCL-R* (2nd ed.). Multi-Health Systems, Inc.

- The second edition of the *Psychopathy Checklist–Revised (PCL-R)*, the gold-standard clinical tool for assessing psychopathy in forensic and research settings. The manual details the instrument's structure, administration, and scoring procedures, capturing both affective–interpersonal and behavioral–lifestyle dimensions of psychopathy. Backed by extensive empirical validation, the PCL-R provides a reliable framework for identifying individuals with pronounced callousness, manipulativeness, and antisocial behavior, shaping decades of research on psychopathic personality and criminal behavior.

Hartford, T. C., Chen, Chiung M., Kerridge, B. T., & Grant, B. F. (2019). Borderline Personality Disorder and Violence Toward Self and Others: A National Study. *Journal of Personality Disorders, 33*(5), 653-670. https://doi.org/10.1521/pedi_2018_32_361

- Analyzed data from a large, nationally representative sample to examine the relationship between borderline personality disorder (BPD) and violent behaviors toward both self and others. The study found that individuals with BPD were at significantly increased risk for self-directed violence (e.g., suicide attempts) as well as interpersonal aggression, even after controlling for comorbid conditions such as substance use and depression. These findings highlight BPD's dual risk profile—marked by both self-destructive and outwardly aggressive tendencies—and underscore the importance of integrated assessment and intervention strategies targeting emotional dysregulation and impulsivity.

Hermann, A. D., & Fuller, R. C. (2018). Grandiose narcissism and religiosity. In A.D. Hermann, A.B. Brunell, & J.D. Foster (Eds.), *Handbook of trait narcissism: Key advances, research methods, and controversies* (pp. 379-387). Springer.

- Explores how grandiose narcissists often engage religion as a vehicle for self-importance, moral superiority, and social validation rather than humility or devotion. Illuminates the motivational overlap between spiritual identity and status-enhancing self-concepts.

Herpertz, S. C., & Bertsch, K. (2022). Neuroscience and personality disorders. In S.K. Huprich (Ed.), *Personality disorders and pathology: Integrating clinical assessment and practice in the DSM-5 and ICD-11 era* (pp. 323-349). American Psychological Association.

- Identifies core neural systems regulating empathy, aggression, and affective attunement in Cluster B disorders. Encourages translational research that connects laboratory paradigms—such as social-threat and moral-judgment tasks—to real-world manifestations of cruelty and relational harm.

Hooley, J. M., & Masland, S. R. (2017). Borderline Personality Disorder. In W.E. Craighead, D.J. Miklowitz, & L. W. craighead (Eds.), *Psychopathology: History, diagnosis, and empirical foundations* (3rd ed., pp. 562-611). Wiley.

- Describes BPD as marked by limbic hyperreactivity and diminished prefrontal control, yielding emotional volatility and interpersonal instability. Integrates neurobiological, familial, and sociocultural factors—including stigma and gender bias—without reducing etiology solely to trauma.

Hopwood, J. H., Mulay, A. L., & Waugh, M. H. (Eds.). (2019). *The DSM-5 alternative model for personality disorders: Integrating multiple paradigms of personality assessment*. Routledge.

- Compiled interdisciplinary perspectives on the DSM-5 Alternative Model for Personality Disorders (AMPD), which reconceptualizes personality pathology dimensionally rather than categorically. The volume integrates trait-based, psychodynamic, interpersonal, and neurobiological paradigms to advance a more comprehensive understanding of personality dysfunction. Contributors discuss the model's clinical utility, empirical validation, and implications for assessment, offering a roadmap for integrating traditional diagnostic systems with emerging dimensional frameworks.

Horsthemke, B. (2018). A Critical View on Transgenerational Epigenetic Inheritance in Humans. *Nature Communications* , *9*(1), . https://doi.org/10.1038/s41467-018-05445-5

- Critically evaluates evidence for transgenerational epigenetic inheritance in humans, arguing that current data do not robustly support the transmission of environmentally induced epigenetic changes across generations. The article distinguishes between true germline inheritance and intergenerational effects mediated by shared environment or parental physiology. By highlighting methodological limitations and misinterpretations in the literature, it calls for more rigorous experimental and longitudinal designs before asserting that acquired traits can be biologically inherited in humans.

Jauk, E., Blum, C., Hildebrandt, M., Lehmann, K., Maliske, L., & Kanske, P. (2024). Psychological and neural correlates of social affect and cognition in narcissism: A multimethod study of self-reported traits, experiential states, and behavioral and brain indicators. *Personality disorders: Theory, research, and treatment, 15*(2), 157-171.

- A multimethod investigation into the psychological and neural correlates of narcissism, integrating self-report measures, behavioral tasks, and neuroimaging data. The study revealed distinct neural activation patterns associated with narcissistic traits, particularly within regions implicated in empathy, social cognition, and self-referential processing, such as the medial prefrontal cortex and temporoparietal junction. Findings demonstrate that narcissism involves both heightened self-focus and diminished affective resonance, supporting a dual model in which interpersonal dysfunction arises from imbalances between self-enhancement and social-affective processing systems.

Jauk, E., & Kanske, P. (2021). Can neuroscience help to understand narcissism? A systematic review of an emerging field. *Personal Neuroscience, .* https://doi.org/10.1017/pen.2021.1

- Systematically reviews neuroimaging evidence implicating self-referential, empathy, and reward-processing networks in narcissism. Concludes that narcissism arises from dysregulated large-scale brain network functioning rather than localized abnormalities, integrating cognitive-affective and neurobiological perspectives.

Kendler, K. S., & Baker, J. H. (2007). Genetic influences on measures of the environment: A systematic review. *Psychological Medicine, 37*(5), 615–626. https://doi.org/10.1017/S0033291706009524

A systematic review of twin and adoption studies examining how genetic factors influence ostensibly environmental measures such as life events, parenting, and social support. The meta-analysis reveals that environmental exposures commonly assumed to be independent of biology show significant heritability. The findings underscore the concept of gene–environment correlation, suggesting that individuals partially shape their own environments through genetically influenced traits and behaviors.

Kiehl, K. (2014). *The psychopath whisperer: The science of those without conscience*. Broadway Books.

- Presents decades of neuroimaging and forensic research positioning psychopathy as a neurodevelopmental condition marked by paralimbic dysfunction. Provides accessible scientific insight into deficits in empathy, moral reasoning, and affective processing underlying antisocial and exploitative behavior.

Krizan, Z. (2018). The narcissism spectrum model: A spectrum perspective on narcissistic personality. In A. D. Hermann, A. B. Brunell, & J. D. Foster (Eds.), *Handbook of trait narcissism: Key advances, research methods, and controversies* (pp. 15-25). Springer International Publishing.

- Introduces the Narcissism Spectrum Model (NSM), which conceptualizes narcissism as a continuum anchored by self-enhancement and entitlement, spanning from adaptive confidence to pathological grandiosity and vulnerability. The chapter integrates clinical, personality, and social psychological research to explain how antagonism and self-regulation processes shape narcissistic expression. This framework bridges competing theories by situating narcissism along a single dimension encompassing both overt and covert forms of the trait.

Krueger, R. F. (2019). Criterion B of the AMPD and the interpersonal, multivariate, and empirical paradigms of personality assessment. In C.J. Hopwood, A.L. Mulay, & Mark H. Waugh (Eds.), *The DSM-5 alternative model for personality disorders: Integrating multiple paradigms of personality assessment* (pp. 60-76). Routledge.

- Discusses Criterion B of the DSM-5 Alternative Model for Personality Disorders (AMPD), which captures maladaptive trait dimensions across personality pathology. Situates Criterion B within empirical and multivariate paradigms, emphasizing its alignment with contemporary trait psychology and the Five-Factor Model. The chapter argues that dimensional assessment offers a more valid and integrative framework for conceptualizing personality disorder traits than traditional categorical diagnoses.

Linehan, M. M. (1993). *Cognitive behavioral treatment of borderline personality disorder*. The Guilford Press.

- Presents the foundational manual for Dialectical Behavior Therapy (DBT), a structured cognitive-behavioral approach designed for individuals with borderline personality disorder. The text outlines principles of mindfulness, distress tolerance, emotion regulation, and interpersonal effectiveness, integrating acceptance and change strategies. DBT has since become one of the most empirically supported treatments for BPD, effectively reducing self-harm, suicidality, and emotional instability.

Livesley, W. J., & Jang, K. L. (2008). The behavioral genetics of personality disorder. *Annual Review of Clinical Psychology, 4*247-274.

- Synthesizes behavioral genetic evidence demonstrating that personality disorders are highly heritable, with genetic factors accounting for 40–60% of variance across most disorders. The review emphasizes that the same genetic mechanisms underlying normal personality traits also contribute to maladaptive personality configurations. The review highlights gene–environment interplay and developmental continuity, framing personality disorders as quantitative extremes on heritable personality dimensions rather than discrete diagnostic entities.

Luo, Y. L. , & Cai, H. (2018). The etiology of narcissism: A review of behavioral genetic studies. In Anthony D. Hermann, Amy B. Brunell, & Joshua D. Foster (Eds.), *Handbook of trait narcissism: Key advances, research methods, and controversies* (pp. 149-156). Springer International Publishing.

- Synthesizes twin and behavioral-genetic studies revealing moderate-to-high heritability of narcissistic traits (40–60%). Highlights the additive and interactive effects of genes and environment, reframing narcissism as an inherited temperament modulated by developmental context.

Luo, Y. L., Cai, H., & Song, H. (2014). A behavioral genetic study of intrapersonal and interpersonal dimensions of narcissism. *Plos One, 9*(4), . https://doi.org/10.1371/journal.pone.0093403

- A behavioral genetic twin study to examine the heritability of narcissism's intrapersonal (self-enhancement) and interpersonal (exploitativeness) dimensions. The results showed that both dimensions are substantially heritable, with genetic factors accounting for approximately 40–60% of variance, while shared environmental influences were negligible. These findings support the view that narcissism is a stable, biologically rooted personality configuration shaped primarily by genetic predispositions rather than family environment or social learning alone.

Luyten, P., & Fonagy, P. (2018). The neurobiology of attachment and mentalizing: A neurodevelopmental perspective. In C. Schmahl, K. L. Phan, R.O. Friedel, L. J. Siever (Ed.), *Neurobiology of Personalit Disorders* (pp. 111-130). Oxford University Press.

- Links early attachment and mentalization processes to neural network development, emphasizing stress regulation, empathy, and identity integration. Provides a biological bridge between relational trauma and enduring personality dysfunction.

Ma, G., Fan, H., Shen, C., & Wang, W. (2016). Genetic and neuroimaging features of personality disorders: State of the art. *Neuroscience Bulletin, 32*(3), 286-306.

- Reviews genetic and imaging data across major personality disorders, identifying consistent fronto-limbic and prefrontal abnormalities. Advocates for multi-modal research integrating neural and genetic biomarkers to refine nosology and prediction.

Mark, D., Roy, S., Walsh, H., & Neumann, C. S. (2022). Antisocial personality disorder. In S. K. Huprich (Ed.), *Personality disorders and pathology: Integrating clinical assessment and practice in the DSM-5 and ICD-11 era* (pp. 391-411). American Psychological Association. https://doi.org/10.1037/0000310-018

- Provides an updated synthesis of antisocial personality disorder across DSM-5-TR and ICD-11 frameworks, delineating its overlap yet distinction from psychopathy. Emphasizes that ASPD is defined primarily by behavioral deviance, whereas psychopathy captures affective and interpersonal callousness—key distinctions for forensic and risk-management contexts.

Matteson, L., & McGue, M. (2020). Development of personality in adulthood: A behavioral genetical perspective. In K.J. Saudino & J.M. Ganiban (Eds.), *Behavior genetics of temperament and personality* (pp. 41-74). Springer International Publishing.

- Reviews behavioral genetic research on the development and stability of personality across adulthood. Drawing on longitudinal twin studies, the review demonstrates that while personality traits remain moderately stable over time, both genetic and nonshared environmental influences contribute to individual differences and age-related change. The chapter emphasizes dynamic gene–environment interplay—showing that genetic factors guide personality continuity, whereas unique life experiences shape developmental adaptation—offering a lifespan perspective on the biological and experiential foundations of personality.

Meloy, J. R., & Reavis, J. A. (2007). The dangerous cases: When treatment is not an option. In J.B. Van Luyn, S. Akhtar, & J. Livesley (Eds.), *Severe personality disorders: Everday issues in clinical practice* (pp. 181-195). Cambridge University Press. https://doi.org/10.1017/CBO9780511544439.012

- Addresses clinical management of treatment-refractory cases marked by sadism, dominance, and psychopathy. Discusses ethical, forensic, and countertransference challenges in settings where therapy may reinforce manipulation or danger.

Meyer-Lindenberg, A., Buckholtz, J. W., Kolachana, B., Hariri, A. R., Pezawas, L., Blasi, G., Wabnitz, A., Honea, R., Verchinski, B., Callicott, J. H., Egan, M., Mattay, V., & Weinberger, D. R. (2006). Neural mechanisms of genetic risk for impulsivity and violence in humans. *Proceedings of the National Academy of Sciences of the United States of America, 103*(16), 6269–6274. https://doi.org/10.1073/pnas.0511311103

- This study investigates how genetic variation in the monoamine oxidase A (MAOA) gene influences neural circuits linked to impulsivity and aggression. Using fMRI, the study found that individuals with the low-activity MAOA variant exhibited increased amygdala reactivity and decreased regulatory activation in the prefrontal cortex during emotional processing. The findings provide neurobiological evidence that genetic predispositions can heighten vulnerability to violent and impulsive behavior through altered limbic–prefrontal connectivity.

Miles, G. J., & Francis, A. J. (2014). Narcissism: Is parenting style to blame, or is their X-chromosome involvement? *Psychiatry Research, 219*712-713.

- Examines competing explanations for the development of narcissistic traits, contrasting psychosocial models emphasizing parenting style with emerging evidence of biological influences, including potential X-chromosome involvement. The authors argue that while parental overindulgence and inconsistent boundaries may shape expression, genetic mechanisms likely contribute to underlying narcissistic predispositions. Their report highlights the need for integrative research that considers

both inherited and environmental pathways in the
etiology of narcissism.

Miller, J. D., & Campbell, W. K. (2010). The case for using research on
    trait narcissism as a building block for understanding narcissistic
    personality disorder. *personality disorders: Theory, research, and
    treatment, 1*(3), 180-191.

- Argues that dimensional trait models better capture the
  continuum from normative self-focus to pathological
  narcissism. Shows strong structural and etiological
  continuity between subclinical narcissism and DSM-
  defined NPD.

Miller, J. D., Crowe, M. L., & Sharpe, B. M. (2022). Narcissism and the
    DSM-5 alternative model of personality disorder. *Personality disor-
    ders: Theory, research, and treatment, 13*(4), 407-411.

- Applies the AMPD framework to narcissism, aligning
  grandiosity with antagonism and vulnerability with
  negative affectivity. Provides clarity on how narcissistic
  pathology maps onto dimensional trait domains.

Miller, J. D., Lynam, D. R., Hyatt, C. S., & Campbell, W. K. (2017).
    Controversies in narcissism. *Annual Review of Clinical Psychology,
    13*291-315.

- Synthesizes ongoing debates about the structure,
  adaptiveness, and measurement of narcissism. Advocates
  integrative approaches combining personality, social, and
  clinical psychology to reconcile fragmented models.

Miller, J. D., Widiger, T. A., & Campbell, W. K. (2014). Vulnerable
    narcissism: Commentary for the special series "Narcissistic Person-
    ality Disorder - New Perspectives on Diagnosis and Treatment".
    personality disorders: Theory, research, and treatment, 5(4), 450-451.

- Argues that "vulnerable narcissism" remains a narcissistic subtype, not a separate construct, due to shared antagonistic and self-centered features. Challenges purely shame-based conceptualizations that obscure underlying entitlement and grandiosity.

Millon, T., Millon, C. M., Meagher, S. E., Grossman, S. D., & Ramnath, R. (2004). *Personality disorders in modern life*(2nd ed.). Wiley.

- This comprehensive volume integrates theoretical, clinical, and empirical perspectives on the classification, etiology, and treatment of personality disorders. The authors present an evolutionary–biopsychosocial model that conceptualizes personality pathology as maladaptive variants of normal personality styles. The text remains a foundational reference in clinical psychology, emphasizing multidimensional assessment, comorbidity, and treatment approaches grounded in Millon's influential model of personality development and disorder.

Mitchell, K. J. (2018). *Innate: How the wiring of our brains shapes who we are*. Princeton University Press.

- Explores how genetic variability and neural wiring underlie individuality in cognition, temperament, and psychopathology. Refutes genetic determinism, emphasizing plasticity and environmental modulation of biological predispositions.

Mukherjee, S. (2017). *The gene: An intimate history*. Scribner.

- Chronicles the history of genetics and its moral, scientific, and societal implications. Offers a balanced

discussion of heredity, identity, and the ethical
boundaries of biological explanation.

Munoz Centifanti, L. C., Thomson, N. D., & Kwok, A. H. (2016).
Identifying the manipulative mating methods associated with
psychopathic traits and BPD features. *Journal of Personality Disorders, 30*(6), 241-271. https://doi.org/10.1521/pedi_2015_29_225

- Finds that psychopathic traits predict calculated,
deceptive mating tactics, whereas BPD features are tied to
retaliatory and emotionally charged seduction.
Underscores the intentional and strategic components of
sexual and relational exploitation beyond mere
impulsivity explanations.

Nelson, R. J., & Kriegsfeld, L. J. (2018). *An introduction to behavioral
endocrinology* (5th ed.). Oxford University Press.

- Provides a comprehensive overview of the interactions
between hormones, brain function, and behavior across
species, integrating findings from neuroscience, psychology,
and physiology. The text examines how endocrine systems
influence emotion, aggression, reproduction, and social
behavior, emphasizing the bidirectional relationship
between hormonal activity and environmental context.
This foundational work bridges biological and behavioral
sciences, offering critical insight into the neuroendocrine
mechanisms underlying personality and psychopathology.

Nenadic, I., Lorenz, C., & Gaser, C. (2021). Narcissistic personality
traits and prefrontal brain structure. *Scientific Reports, 11*. https://
doi.org/10.1038s41598-021-94920-z

- Used voxel-based morphometry to investigate structural
brain correlates of narcissistic personality traits. The

study found that higher narcissism scores were associated with reduced gray matter volume in prefrontal regions implicated in empathy, self-regulation, and moral reasoning. These findings provide neuroanatomical evidence linking narcissistic traits to diminished prefrontal integrity, supporting theories that associate narcissism with deficits in emotional control and interpersonal attunement.

Nikolova, S. Y., Davis, G. E., & Hariri, A. R. (2018). Genetic contributions to affection and emotion. In L.F. Barrett, M. Lewis, & J.M. Haviland-Jones (Eds.), *Handbook of emotions* (4th ed., pp. 182-198). The Guilford Press.

- Reviews gene–emotion research implicating serotonergic and dopaminergic polymorphisms in affective regulation. Positions emotion as a heritable neurobiological system influencing temperament and personality vulnerability.

Paris, J. (2015). *A concise guide to personality disorders*. American Psychological Association.

- An accessible yet scholarly overview of the major personality disorders, integrating findings from genetics, neurobiology, and clinical research. The book challenges trauma-exclusive models by emphasizing the temperamental and heritable components underlying personality pathology and provides concise guidance on diagnosis, prognosis, and evidence-based treatment, framing personality disorders as stable, biologically influenced patterns of behavior that interact with environmental stressors across the lifespan.

Paris, J. (2023). *Myths of Trauma: Why adversity does not necessarily make us sick*. Oxford University Press.

- Argues that adversity influences symptom expression but rarely causes personality disorder etiology outright. Challenges trauma-exclusive narratives by emphasizing temperament, heritability, and probabilistic vulnerability rather than deterministic injury models.

Paris, J. (2025). *A concise guide to borderline personality disorder*. American Psychological Association.

- Synthesizes contemporary findings in genetics, neurobiology, and psychosocial adaptation to explain BPD as a disorder of affective dysregulation rooted in temperament. Clarifies that effective interventions emphasize structured skill acquisition (e.g., DBT) over curative psychotherapy.

Paulhus, D. L., & Williams, K. M. (2002). The Dark Triad of personality: Narcissism, Machiavellianism, and psychopathy. *Journal of Research in Personality, 36*(6), 556–563. https://doi.org/10.1016/S0092-6566(02)00505-6

- Introduces the concept of the *Dark Triad*, describing narcissism, Machiavellianism, and psychopathy as three interrelated yet distinct personality constructs marked by callousness, manipulation, and self-interest. Through empirical analysis, the authors demonstrate moderate correlations among the traits, supporting their shared antagonistic core while highlighting their unique motivational and interpersonal features. This seminal study established a foundational framework for subsequent research on socially aversive personality traits and their behavioral and relational consequences.

Petrosino, A., MacDougall, P., Hollis-Peel, M. E., Fronius, T. A., & Guckenburg, S. (2015). Antisocial behavior of children and adolescents: Harmful treatments, effective interventions, and novel strategies. In S.O. Lilienfeld, S.J. Lynn, & J.M. Lohr (Eds.), *The science and pseudoscience in clinical psychology* (2nd ed., pp. 500-532). The Guilford Press.

- Review of the empirical evidence on interventions for antisocial behavior in children and adolescents, distinguishing between harmful, ineffective, and evidence-based approaches. The authors highlight how certain punitive or coercive treatments—such as boot camps or "Scared Straight" programs—can exacerbate antisocial tendencies, whereas structured cognitive-behavioral and family-based interventions show strong efficacy. The chapter underscores the importance of grounding youth treatment strategies in rigorous scientific evidence, advocating for preventive and rehabilitative models over deterrence-based or pseudoscientific methods.

Petrosino, A., Turpin-Petrosino, C., & Guckenburg, S. (2010). *Formal system processing of juveniles: Effects on delinquency* (Campbell Systematic Reviews, Vol. 6, Issue 1, pp. 1–88). Campbell Collaboration. https://doi.org/10.4073/csr.2010.1

- A systematic review of 29 experimental studies published between 1973 and 2008 to evaluate whether formal juvenile justice processing reduces recidivism. Their meta-analysis found no evidence of deterrent effects; instead, system involvement was often associated with *increased* delinquent behavior compared to diversion or nonintervention. The authors conclude that traditional juvenile justice processing fails to produce crime-control benefits and may exacerbate offending, emphasizing the need for policy reform and evidence-based alternatives to formal adjudication.

Plomin, R. (2019). *Blueprint: How DNA makes us who we are*. The MIT Press.

- Integrates decades of behavioral-genetic research showing that inherited DNA differences account for substantial variance in personality, intelligence, and psychopathology. The book demonstrates that heritability accounts for roughly half of the variance in personality and that environmental effects are largely unsystematic ("the luck of the draw") rather than deterministic. Plomin contends that understanding genetic influence is essential for realistic models of development and for dispelling the myth that upbringing alone shapes who we become.

Polderman, T. J., Benyamin, B., De Leeuw, C. A., Sullivan, P. F., Van Bochoven, A., Visscher, P. M., & Posthuma, D. (2015). Meta-analyses of the heritability of human traits based on fifty years of twin studies. *Nature Genetics, 47*(7), 702-712.

- Comprehensive synthesis of over 2,700 twin studies confirming an average heritability of roughly 49 percent across human traits, including psychopathology. Provides a robust quantitative anchor against trauma-only etiological claims and supports dimensional genetic architectures of personality.

Ramsland, K. (2016). *Confession of a serial killer: The untold story of Dennis Radar, the BTK killer*. ForeEdge.

- In-depth psychological case study illustrating sadism and instrumental cruelty in the absence of documented trauma. Reinforces the view that deliberate harm stems from dispositional callousness and volitional control rather than reactive pain, underscoring cruelty as an enacted choice within innate predisposition.

Reich, D. (2018). *Who we are and how we got here: Ancient DNA and the new science of the human past*. Vintage Books.

- Synthesizes groundbreaking research from ancient DNA studies to trace human evolutionary history and population migration patterns. By analyzing genomic data from ancient remains, the book reveals how genetic admixture shaped modern human diversity and behavioral variation. This work challenges simplistic notions of ancestry and identity, illustrating how advances in population genetics illuminate the biological and evolutionary roots of human traits—including those influencing temperament and social behavior.

Reichborn-Kjennerud, T. (2010). The genetic epidemiology of personality disorders. *Dialogues in Clinical Neuroscience, 12*(1), 103-114.

- Reviews twin and family studies examining the heritability and genetic structure of personality disorders. The findings indicate that all major personality disorders show moderate to high heritability, with genetic factors explaining a substantial proportion of individual differences in core traits such as neuroticism, antagonism, and disinhibition. The review highlights that genetic risk overlaps across diagnostic categories, supporting dimensional models of personality pathology and underscoring gene–environment interplay in the expression of these disorders.

Reichborn-Kjennerud, T., & Kendler, K. S. (2018). Genetics of personality disorders. In C. Schmahl, K. L. Phan, R.O. Friedel, & L.J. Siever (Eds.), *Neurobiology of Personality Disorders* (pp. 57-73). Oxford University Press.

- Provides an overview of the genetic foundations of personality disorders, synthesizing evidence from twin,

family, and molecular genetic studies. They report
consistent heritability estimates across disorders—
typically ranging from 40% to 60%—and emphasize that
genetic influences are largely shared across diagnostic
boundaries rather than unique to individual disorders.
The chapter situates these findings within emerging
molecular research, highlighting gene–environment
correlations, polygenic risk factors, and the dimensional
nature of personality pathology within contemporary
neurobiological models.

Rice, M. E., Harris, G. T., & Cormier, C. A. (1992). An evaluation of a
maximum security therapeutic community for psychopaths and
other mentally disordered offenders. Law and Human Behavior,
16(4), 399–412. https://doi.org/10.1007/BF02352266

- Evaluated the outcomes of a therapeutic community
  program for psychopathic and other mentally disordered
  offenders in a maximum-security setting. The
  longitudinal data revealed that psychopathic participants
  not only failed to benefit from treatment but also showed
  higher rates of violent recidivism compared to untreated
  controls. The study became pivotal in shaping clinical
  and correctional perspectives on psychopathy, suggesting
  that traditional therapeutic approaches may
  inadvertently reinforce manipulative and antisocial
  behaviors in this population.

Ringwald, W. R., Emery, L., Khoo, S., Clark, L. A., Kotelnikova, Y.,
Scalco, M. D., Watson, D., Wright, A. G., & Simms, L. J. (2023).
Structure of pathological personality traits through the lens of the
CAT-PD model. Assessment, 30(7), 2276-2295.

- Applies the Computerized Adaptive Test of Personality
  Disorder (CAT-PD) framework to examine the
  hierarchical structure of pathological personality traits.

Findings support a multidimensional model aligning closely with established trait domains such as negative affectivity, antagonism, disinhibition, and detachment. The study provides strong empirical validation for the CAT-PD as an efficient, psychometrically robust tool for assessing maladaptive traits across the continuum from normal personality to clinical pathology.

Roberts, B. W., Kuncel, N. R., Shiner, R., Caspi, A., & Goldberg, L. R. (2007). The power of personality: The comparative validity of personality traits, socioeconomic status, and cognitive ability for predicting important life outcomes. *Perspectives in Psychological Science, 2*(4), 313-345.

- A meta-analytic review comparing the predictive power of personality traits with socioeconomic status (SES) and cognitive ability across major life domains such as work performance, health, and longevity. The results showed that personality traits—particularly conscientiousness and emotional stability—predict important life outcomes as strongly as or more strongly than SES or IQ. The study underscores personality's central role in shaping life trajectories, supporting trait-based approaches to understanding human adaptation and functioning.

Ruocco, A. C., Medaglia, J. D., Tinker, J. R., Ayaz, H., Forman, E. M., Newman, C. F., Williams, J. M., Hillary, F. G., Platek, S. M., Onaral, B., & Chute, D. L. (2010). Medial prefrontal cortex hyper-activation during social exclusion in borderline personality disorder. *Psychiatry Research: Neuroimaging, 181*(3), 233–236. https://doi.org/10.1016/j.pscychresns.2009.12.001

- Used neuroimaging to investigate brain activation patterns in individuals with borderline personality disorder (BPD) during experiences of social exclusion.

The study found hyperactivation of the medial prefrontal cortex, confirming amygdala hyperreactivity and frontolimbic dysregulation during social threat processing in BPD. These findings provide biological grounding for the claim that BPD involves pathological threat detection—not merely emotional sensitivity—integrating neuroscientific evidence with clinical observation of interpersonal hypersensitivity and instability.

Russell, G. A. (1985). Narcissism and the narcissistic personality disorder: A comparison of the theories of Kernberg and Kohut. *British Journal of Medical Psychology, 58*137-148.

- Compares the theoretical frameworks of Otto Kernberg and Heinz Kohut regarding narcissism and narcissistic personality disorder (NPD). The paper contrasts Kernberg's object-relations view—emphasizing aggression, pathological internalized object relations, and defensive grandiosity—with Kohut's self-psychological model, which centers on deficits in self-cohesion and empathic attunement. Russell provides a balanced analysis highlighting both the complementarity and tension between these perspectives, illustrating how differing developmental and structural assumptions inform modern psychodynamic understanding of narcissism.

Sanchez-Roige, S., Fontanillas, P., Elson, S. L., 23andMe Research Team, Pandit, A., Schmidt, E. M., Foerster, J. R., Abecasis, G. R., Gray, J. C., de Wit, H., Davis, L. K., MacKillop, J., & Palmer, A. A. (2018). Genome-wide association study of delay discounting in 23,217 adult research participants of European ancestry. *Nature Neuroscience, 21*(1), 16–18. https://doi.org/10.1038/s41593-017-0032-x

- Large-scale genome-wide association study (GWAS) to identify genetic correlates of delay discounting—the tendency to prefer smaller immediate rewards over larger delayed ones. Analyzing data from over 23,000 participants, the study revealed significant heritability and identified specific single nucleotide polymorphisms (SNPs) associated with impulsivity-related decision-making. The findings establish delay discounting as a quantifiable behavioral phenotype with measurable genetic underpinnings, linking impulsivity to broader neurobiological and psychiatric risk pathways.

Sanchez-Roige, S., Gray, J. C., MacKillop, J. K., & Palmer, A. A. (2018). The genetics of human personality. *Genes, Brain, & Behavior, 17*(3), . https://doi.org/10.1111/gbb.12439.

- Review of molecular genetic studies identifying biological underpinnings of human personality traits. The authors summarize evidence from genome-wide association studies (GWAS) linking personality dimensions—such as neuroticism, extraversion, and impulsivity—to polygenic architectures involving dopaminergic and serotonergic pathways. The article emphasizes that personality arises from complex, additive genetic effects interacting with environmental influences, providing a biological framework for understanding stable individual differences in behavior and temperament.

Santana, E. J. (2016). The brain of the psychopath: A systematic review of structural neuroimaging studies. *Psychology & Neuroscience, 9*(4), 420-443.

- Systematic review of structural neuroimaging research on psychopathy, identifying consistent reductions in gray matter volume within the prefrontal cortex, amygdala, and paralimbic regions. The review supports a neurobiological model of psychopathy characterized by deficits in emotional regulation, empathy, and moral reasoning. By synthesizing findings across multiple imaging modalities, the paper provides robust evidence that psychopathic traits are linked to distinct and measurable abnormalities in brain morphology.

Schmahl, C., Luan Phan, K., Friedel, R. O., & Siever, L. J. (Eds.). (2018). *Neurobiology of Personality Disorders*. Oxford.

- Comprehensive reference synthesizing genetic, neurochemical, and neurocircuitry data on personality disorders. Establishes biological models linking temperament, affective instability, and neural structure to enduring maladaptive traits.

Shulze, L., Dziobek, I., Vater, A., Heekeren, H. R., Bajbouj, M., Renneberg, B., Heuser, I., & Roepke, S. (2013). Gray matter abnormalities in patients with narcissistic personality disorder. *Journal of Psychiatric Research, 47*(10), 1363-1369.

- Used voxel-based morphometry to examine structural brain differences in individuals diagnosed with narcissistic personality disorder (NPD). The study identified reduced gray matter volume in regions associated with empathy, emotion regulation, and self-referential processing, including the anterior insula and prefrontal cortex. These neuroanatomical findings provide biological evidence of impaired emotional resonance and self-regulatory capacity in NPD, supporting models that conceptualize narcissism as rooted in fronto-limbic dysfunction rather than purely psychological or developmental factors.

Simon, Jr., G. (2010). *In sheep's clothing: understanding and dealing with manipulative people* (Rev. ed.). Parkhurst Brothers Publishers.

- A practical exploration of covert aggression and manipulative behavior, introducing the concept of "covert-aggressive personalities" who control others through deception, guilt induction, and subtle domination. Drawing from clinical and real-world examples, the book distinguishes character disturbance from neurotic conflict and emphasizes accountability over victim empathy in managing manipulative individuals. It remains an influential resource for understanding personality-driven abuse and interpersonal exploitation outside traditional diagnostic frameworks.

Simon, Jr., G. K. (2011). *Character disturbance: The phenomenon of our age*. Parkhurst Brothers Publishers.

- Expands on the psychology of disordered character, arguing that societal permissiveness and moral relativism have contributed to a rise in manipulative, entitled, and remorseless personality patterns. The book bridges clinical insight with cultural commentary, distinguishing character disturbance from traditional neurosis and offering strategies for recognizing and confronting manipulative behaviors. It serves as both a psychological and ethical examination of modern antisociality and narcissism.

South, S. C., & DeYoung, N. J. (2013). Behavior genetics of personality disorders: Informing classification and conceptualization in DSM-5. *Personality disorders: Theory, research, and treatment, 4*(3), 270-283.

- Review of behavioral genetic findings that inform the DSM-5's dimensional approach to personality disorders.

Synthesizing twin and molecular studies, they report moderate to high heritability estimates across personality disorder clusters and highlight the overlap between normal trait dimensions and pathological variants. The authors argue that genetic data support a dimensional, trait-based taxonomy of personality pathology, aligning with the DSM-5 Alternative Model and advancing biological validity in classification.

South, S. C., Reichborn-Kjennerud, T., Eaton, N. R., & Krueger, R. F. (2013). Behavior and Molecular Genetics of Personality Disorders. In T.A. Widiger (Ed.), *Oxford handbook of personality disorders* (1st ed., pp. 143-160). Oxford University Press.

- Summarizes advances in behavioral and molecular genetics as they pertain to personality disorders. The chapter outlines consistent heritability estimates and discusses how shared genetic factors contribute to comorbidity among disorders. Integrating molecular findings with trait-based models, the authors propose that genetic research supports viewing personality disorders as extreme variants of normal personality structure, reinforcing dimensional and biologically informed classification systems.

Streit, F., Witt, S. H., Awasthi, S., Foo, J. C., Jungkunz, M., Frank, J., Colodro-Conde, L., Hindley, G., Smeland, O. B., Maslahati, T., Schware, C. E., & Dahmen, N. (2022). Borderline personality disorder and the big five: molecular genetic analyses indicated shared genetic architecture with neuroticism and openness. *Translational Psychiatry, 12*(153), . https://doi.org/10.1038/s41398-022-01912-2

- Presents genome-wide evidence of overlapping genetic architecture between BPD and major personality traits. Strengthens dimensional, polygenic models of personality disorder etiology and classification.

Torgersen, S., Lygren, S., Oien, P. A., S, I., Onstad, S., Edvardsen, J., Tambs, K., & Kringlen, E. (2000). A twin study of personality disorders. *Comprehensive Psychiatry, 41*(6), 416-425.

- One of the most comprehensive twin studies on personality disorders, using structured diagnostic interviews to assess heritability across DSM-defined categories. The study found significant genetic contributions to all personality disorder clusters, with heritability estimates averaging around 40–60%, particularly high for Cluster B disorders such as antisocial and borderline personality disorder. Shared environmental influences were negligible, indicating that individual-specific environments and genetic factors primarily account for the development of personality pathology. These findings provided foundational evidence for the biological basis of personality disorders and influenced subsequent behavioral genetic research.

Torgersen, S., Myers, J., Rechborn-Kjennerud, T., Roysamb, E., Kubarych, T. S., & Kendler, K. S. (2013). The heritability of Cluster B personality disorders assessed by personal interview and questionnaire. *Journal of Personality Disorders, 26*(6), 848-866. https://doi.org/10.1521/pedi.2012.26.6.848

- Examined genetic and environmental contributions to Cluster B personality disorders using data from approximately 2,800 twins in the Norwegian Institute of Public Health Twin Panel. Participants completed both a self-report questionnaire and, years later, the Structured Interview for DSM-IV Personality (SIDP-IV). By combining these data through measurement models fitted in Mx, the researchers found that heritability estimates were around .69 for antisocial (APD), .67 for borderline (BPD), .71 for narcissistic (NPD), and .63 for histrionic (HPD). As is typical for personality traits, shared familial environmental effects were negligible, confirming that genetic factors, rather than upbringing, account for most of the variance in Cluster B personality pathology.

Treadway, M. T., & Zald, D. H. (2013). Parsing anhedonia: Translational models of reward-processing deficits in psychopathology. *Current Directions in Psychological Science, 22*(3), 244–249. https://doi.org/10.1177/0963721412474460

- Synthesizes human and animal research on dopaminergic reward circuits, distinguishing motivational ("wanting") deficits from consummatory ("liking") deficits in anhedonia. Their translational framework clarifies how disrupted reward processing contributes to diminished motivation and pleasure across psychiatric conditions. These insights can be extrapolated to explain compensatory reward-seeking behaviors—such as thrill-seeking, dominance, and risk-taking—often observed in Cluster B personality traits.

Tuvblad, C., & Beaver, K. M. (2013). Genetic and environmental influences on antisocial behavior. *Journal of Criminal Justice, 41*(5), 273–276. https://doi.org/10.1016/j.jcrimjus.2013.07.007

- This review synthesizes behavioral genetic research on the development of antisocial behavior across the lifespan. The review highlights consistent evidence from twin and adoption studies demonstrating substantial heritability, alongside moderating environmental influences such as parenting and peer context. The authors emphasize that antisocial behavior results from complex gene–environment interplay, challenging purely social or environmental explanations for criminality.

Van Den Berg, S. M., & De Moor, M. H. (2020). Molecular genetic research on personality. In K.J. Saudino and J.M. Ganiban (Ed.), *Behavior genetics of temperament and personality* (pp. 99-121). Springer International .

  • Review of advances in molecular genetics that have deepened understanding of the biological foundations of personality. Summarizing evidence from genome-wide association studies (GWAS), the review highlights that personality traits are highly polygenic, influenced by thousands of genetic variants each exerting small additive effects. The authors emphasize the emerging role of polygenic risk scores in linking molecular data to personality theory, underscoring how genetics complements psychological and environmental models of personality development.

Vitale, J. E., & Newman, J. P. (2017). Psychopathy as psychopathology: Key developments in assessment, etiology, and treatment. In *Psychopathology: History, diagnosis, and empirical foundations* (3rd ed., pp. 612-650). Wiley.

  • Provides a comprehensive overview of psychopathy as a clinical construct, examining its historical development, neurobiological underpinnings, and implications for treatment. The chapter synthesizes evidence linking psychopathy to deficits in emotion processing, reward sensitivity, and behavioral inhibition, grounded in empirical assessment tools such as the PCL-R. The authors argue that psychopathy represents a distinct form of psychopathology characterized by affective and interpersonal deficits rather than antisocial behavior alone, guiding both diagnostic understanding and intervention strategies.

Waller, R., & Hyde, L. W. (2017). callous-unemotional behaviors in early childhood: Measurement, meaning, and the influence of parenting. *Child Developmental Perspectives , 11*(2), 120-126.

- Review of research on callous-unemotional (CU) behaviors in young children, focusing on their reliable measurement, developmental significance, and environmental correlates. The authors highlight that CU traits—marked by low empathy, guilt, and affective responsiveness—emerge early in life and are moderately heritable. They also note that positive, warm, and consistent parenting can mitigate risk, underscoring the importance of early intervention and the dynamic interplay between genetic vulnerability and caregiving environment in the development of antisocial behavior.

Walsh, Z., & Kosson, D. S. (2008). Psychopathy and violence: The importance of factor level interactions. *Psychological Assessment, 20*(2), 114–120. https://doi.org/10.1037/1040-3590.20.2.114

- Examines how distinct dimensions of psychopathy interact to predict violent behavior. Their findings show that the combination of affective–interpersonal traits (e.g., callousness, manipulativeness) and impulsive–antisocial traits confers the highest risk for violence, underscoring the heterogeneity within psychopathy. The study highlights the need to assess psychopathic traits at the factor level rather than treating psychopathy as a unitary construct, refining both clinical assessment and risk prediction models.

Wang, Z., & Deater-Deckard, K. (2020). Gene-environment processes linking temperament and parenting. In K.J. Saudino & J.M. Ganiban (Eds.), *Behavior genetics of temperament and personality* (pp. 263-300). Springer International Publishing.

- Explores how genetic and environmental factors jointly shape the dynamic relationship between temperament and parenting. Drawing on behavioral genetic and developmental research, the authors describe how children's heritable temperamental traits can evoke specific parenting responses (evocative gene–environment correlation) and how parents' own genetically influenced characteristics affect caregiving behavior. The chapter emphasizes bidirectional influences and gene–environment interplay, illustrating how temperament and parenting co-develop over time to influence personality formation and behavioral outcomes.

Weiss, B., & Miller, J. D. (2018). Distinguishing between grandiose narcissism, vulnerable narcissism, and narcissistic personality disorder. In Anthony D. Hermann, Amy B. Brunell, & Joshua D. Foster (Eds.), *Handbook of trait narcissism: Key advances, research methods, and controversies* (pp. 3-13). Springer International Publishing.

- Clarifies conceptual and empirical differences among grandiose, vulnerable, and clinical narcissism. Proposes a unified framework grounded in antagonism, entitlement, and self-importance as the disorder's core features.

Widiger, T. A., & Crego, C. (2019). The Five Factor Model of personality structure: An update. *World Psychiatry, 18*(3), 271–272. https://doi.org/10.1002/wps.20658

- Provides a concise update on the Five Factor Model (FFM) as a framework for understanding both normal and maladaptive personality variation. Highlights growing consensus that personality disorders can be conceptualized as extreme or pathological variants of the FFM domains—particularly antagonism, disinhibition, and negative affectivity. The article reinforces the dimensional approach adopted in contemporary diagnostic systems, emphasizing the FFM's utility for integrating clinical assessment with trait-based models of personality pathology.

Wilson, N., Robb, E., Gajwani, R., & Minnis, H. (2021). Nature and nurture? A review of the literature on childhood maltreatment and genetic factors in the pathogenesis of borderline personality disorder. *Journal of Psychiatric Research, 137*131-146.

- Review of empirical research examining how childhood maltreatment interacts with genetic vulnerability in the development of borderline personality disorder (BPD). The authors highlight evidence that while early trauma is a significant environmental risk factor, it is neither necessary nor sufficient to cause BPD without underlying heritable predispositions related to emotional dysregulation and impulsivity. The review underscores gene–environment interplay as central to BPD etiology, integrating findings from behavioral genetics, neurobiology, and developmental psychopathology to clarify how biological sensitivity and adverse experiences converge in shaping personality pathology.

Woodworth, M., & Porter, S. (2002). In cold blood: Characteristics of criminal homicides as a function of psychopathy. *Journal of Abnormal Psychology, 111*(3), 436–445. https://doi.org/10.1037/0021-843X.111.3.436

- Analyzed homicide case files to examine how psychopathy influences the nature and motivation of violent crime. Their findings revealed that offenders with high psychopathy scores were significantly more likely to commit *instrumental* (planned, goal-directed) rather than *reactive* (impulsive, affect-driven) homicides. The study provides strong behavioral evidence that psychopathic violence is often strategic and predatory in nature, supporting theoretical models that distinguish psychopathy by its emotional detachment and calculated aggression

Wright, Z. E., Pahlen, S., & Krueger, R. F. (2017). Genetic and environmental influences on diagnostic and statistical manual of mental disorders-fifth edition (DSM-5). maladaptive personality traits and their connections with normative personality traits. *Journal of Abnormal Psychology, 126*(4), 416-428.

- Used twin data to examine the genetic and environmental structure of maladaptive personality traits as defined in the DSM-5, as well as their overlap with normative personality dimensions. The study found that maladaptive and normal traits share substantial genetic variance, indicating that personality pathology represents extreme manifestations of common heritable dispositions. Environmental effects were largely nonshared, reinforcing that individual-specific experiences—rather than shared upbringing—shape the expression of pathological traits. These findings provide strong empirical support for dimensional, trait-based models of personality disorders within the DSM-5 framework.

Yakeley, J. (2018). Current understanding of narcissism and narcissistic personality disorder. *BJPsych Advances, 24*305-315.

- Offers an integrative overview of narcissism and narcissistic personality disorder, tracing the evolution of the construct from classical psychodynamic theories to contemporary neurobiological and clinical models. The article bridges historical and modern perspectives, clarifying how self-regulation, empathy deficits, and interpersonal functioning define the disorder. It provides a clinically grounded synthesis aimed at improving diagnostic clarity and psychotherapeutic engagement with narcissistic patients.

Yudofsky, S. C. (2005). *Fatal Flaws: Navigating destructive relationships with people with disorders of personality and character.* American Psychiatric Association Publishing.

- Offers a clinically informed exploration of destructive relationship patterns involving individuals with personality and character disorders. Drawing on psychiatric case studies and decades of clinical experience, the author distinguishes between disordered personality traits and moral deficits, emphasizing the profound interpersonal and emotional harm such individuals can inflict. The book provides practical strategies for recognizing, managing, and disengaging from toxic relational dynamics, while framing these behaviors within a psychiatric understanding of personality pathology and impaired empathy.

Zimmerman, M. (2023, September). *Overview of personality disorders.* Retrieved March 31, 2024, from https://www.merckmanuals.com/professional/psychiatric-disorders/personality-disorders/overview-of-personality-disorders

- Provides a concise clinical overview of personality disorders in the *Merck Manual*, summarizing their classification, diagnostic criteria, and underlying features. The entry emphasizes enduring, inflexible patterns of cognition, affect, and behavior that cause functional impairment and distress, distinguishing personality disorders from episodic psychiatric conditions. It also discusses etiological factors—including genetic predisposition, temperament, and early developmental influences—offering an accessible synthesis for clinicians and students seeking foundational understanding.

Zwir, I., Arnedo, J., Del-Val, C., Pulkki-Raback, L., Konte, B., Yang, S. S., Romero-Zaliz, R., Hintsanen, M., Cloninger, K. M., Garcia, D., Svrakic, D. M., & Hernandez-Cuervo, H. (2020). Uncovering the complex genetics of human character. *Molecular Psychiatry, 25*2295-2312.

- Conducted a large-scale molecular genetic study to identify genomic networks underlying human character and personality development. Using genome-wide data and multi-trait integration, the researchers discovered that personality-related traits are highly polygenic, influenced by thousands of genetic variants interacting in complex networks linked to brain development, emotion regulation, and social behavior. The study provides compelling evidence that character emerges from coordinated gene clusters affecting both biological and psychosocial adaptation, advancing a systems-genetic model of personality that bridges molecular biology and psychological theory.

If you're in or have been in a relationship with a
pathological personality yet somehow ended up believing

that everything bad was your fault, you're not alone. That's the superpower of disordered personalities: making their victims believe they are in the wrong even when they're not.

Being on the receiving end of chronic but often subtle abuse can be brutal. The result of this dizzying and disorienting up-is-down maelstrom manifested by the pathological personality in your life results in **traumatic cognitive dissonance (TCD)**. This occurs when covert manipulation and other forms of deceit and coercion are experienced on an ongoing basis. TCD represents complex trauma that goes far beyond typical trauma and stress-related symptoms.

But there is help. And knowledge is where it starts. Rest assured that what you have been searching for to make sense of your debilitating situation and to recover once and for all from pathological relationship abuse is right here, between the pages of this book. **Traumatic cognitive dissonance**, when understood, can be over-come. And that's what this book is for—for you to gain the tools and information so you'll be able to reunite with your true sense of self and move forward in your life with a renewed sense of joy. After all you've been through, you deserve it.

THE NATURE *and* NURTURE *of* NARCISSISM

UNDERSTANDING NARCISSISTIC PERSONALITY
DISORDER FROM THE PERSPECTIVE OF GENE-
ENVIRONMENT INTERACTION

PETER SALERNO, PsyD

WHAT CAUSES NARCISSISM?

The world has been indoctrinated with the false notion that narcissism is the result of a bad childhood.

It's as if narcissists have been granted immunity from responsibility. Mental health professionals - and the general public alike - seem more than willing to offer narcissists a perfectly convenient scapegoat: trauma.

The goal of this book, using the most recent empirical evidence on the etiology and treatment of narcissistic personality disorder - is to dispel the widely and *already* discredited myth that narcissism is the result of childhood trauma. Despite evidence to the contrary, this widely held myth continues to prevail in popular media and culture.

This book aims to correct the mistakes related to the cause of narcissism so that mental health practitioners and the general public will have a scientifically informed understanding of etiology and intervention. Because the reality is that almost everything we have been taught about the cause of narcissism...is *wrong*.

recommended readings

Psychopathy and Narcissism

Without Conscience by Robert Hare

A landmark text on psychopathy by the creator of the Hare Psychopathy Checklist (PCL-R). Hare explains how psychopaths think, why they exploit, and how they can be identified.

Snakes in Suits by Robert Hare & Paul Babiak

Focused on the corporate world, this book shows how psychopathic traits manifest in business settings—ambition, charm, manipulation—and the damage they cause in organizations.

The Psychopath Whisperer: The Science of Those Without Conscience by Kent A. Kiehl

A neuroscientist trained under Robert Hare, Kiehl provides a behind-the-scenes look at psychopathy research through his work with incarcerated offenders. He details how neuroimaging reveals structural and functional brain differences in psychopaths, particularly in the paralimbic system. The book balances scientific rigor with accessible storytelling, offering rare insight into the biological underpinnings of conscience, morality, and criminality.

The Sociopath Next Door by Martha Stout

Written for a general audience, Stout describes the everyday sociopath who lacks conscience and uses charm or cruelty to get ahead, often hiding in plain sight.

In Sheep's Clothing by George Simon

A practical guide to recognizing covert aggression and manipulative behavior. Especially useful for survivors trying to understand subtle patterns of control.

Character Disturbance by George Simon

Expands on Simon's earlier work to examine a broad spectrum of disordered personalities, with a focus on accountability and the dangers of excusing harmful behavior.

Run Like Hell by Nadine Macaluso

Memoir and clinical insight from Macaluso, who describes her personal experience with narcissistic abuse and provides a valuable perspective on recovery and resilience.

Framed: Women in the Family Court Underworld by Christine M. Cocchiola & Amy Polacko

Cocchiola and Polacko—both survivors and advocates— share real stories of women who are "framed" in family courts through false allegations, legal weaponization, and systemic bias. The book highlights how abuse dynamics can continue under the guise of legal process and offers a warning, a guide, and a call to reform.

Histrionic Personality Disorder

How to Spot a Histrionic Personality by Joe Navarro

A concise, accessible booklet by former FBI special agent Joe Navarro. Offers a practical checklist of behavioral traits associated with histrionic personality patterns, intended for the lay reader.

Borderline Personality Disorder & High-Conflict Dynamics

Splitting by Bill Eddy & Randi Kreger

Offers strategies for navigating high-conflict relationships with partners who may have borderline or narcissistic traits. Practical and accessible, especially for those facing legal or co-parenting challenges.

A Concise Guide to Borderline Personality Disorder by Joel Paris

An empirically grounded overview of BPD. Paris challenges myths about trauma as the sole cause, emphasizing temperament, biology, and clinical realities.

Genetics, Biology, and Personality

Blueprint by Robert Plomin

A leading behavioral geneticist explains how DNA shapes psychological traits and why genetics play a stronger role than environment in shaping who we are.

Innate by Kevin Mitchell

Explores how genes and brain development interact to produce individual differences in personality and cognition, while also addressing common misunderstandings about determinism.

Born That Way by William Wright

An accessible discussion of the heritability of personality, offering a historical perspective on the nature–nurture debate.

The Gene by Siddhartha Mukherjee

A sweeping narrative of genetic discovery, blending science, history, and biography. Mukherjee traces how our understanding of heredity has shaped medicine and identity.

Rethinking Trauma & Personality in Relationships

Myths of Trauma by Joel Paris

A provocative examination of how trauma has been over-stated as an explanatory model in psychiatry. Paris argues for a more balanced view that recognizes biological and temperamental contributions.

People Problems by Alan Godwin

A clear, accessible book on dealing with difficult personal-ities in everyday life. Godwin outlines patterns of dysfunction and offers practical strategies for navigating them without losing one's own sense of self.

www.ingramcontent.com/pod-product-compliance
Lightning Source LLC
Chambersburg PA
CBHW051622120626
46551CB00014B/1901